How to Manage THE FOUR TYPES of KNOWLEDGE
WORKERS—and **STACK THE ODDS** for Maximum Success

INNOVATORS   MOTIVATORS   ACTIVATORS   IMPLEMENTORS

PLAY YOUR BEST HAND

FAITH RALSTON, PH.D.

Avon, Massachusetts

Dedication

This book is dedicated to my mother Frances Ada Scotchmer,
who gave me this advice when I was a struggling teenager . . .

*"You need to find one thing you do really well,
and everything else will fall into place."*

———————————

Published by
Adams Media, an F+W Publications Company
57 Littlefield Street, Avon, MA 02322. U.S.A.
www.adamsmedia.com

ISBN 10: 1-59337-685-5
ISBN 13: 978-1-59337-685-7

Printed in the United States of America.

J I H G F E D C B A

Library of Congress Cataloging-in-Publication Data
Ralston, Faith.
Play your best hand / Faith Ralston.
        p.   cm.
ISBN-13: 978-1-59337-685-7
ISBN-10: 1-59337-685-5
1. Knowledge workers. 2. Knowledge management. 3. Leadership. I. Title.
HD8039.K59R37 2007
658.4'092—dc22
2006028211

This publication is designed to provide accurate and authoritative information with regard to
the subject matter covered. It is sold with the understanding that the publisher is not engaged
in rendering legal, accounting, or other professional advice. If legal advice or other expert
assistance is required, the services of a competent professional person should be sought.
  —From a *Declaration of Principles* jointly adopted by a Committee of the American Bar
Association and a Committee of Publishers and Associations

Many of the designations used by manufacturers and sellers to distinguish their product are
claimed as trademarks. Where those designations appear in this book and Adams Media was
aware of a trademark claim, the designations have been printed with initial capital letters.

*This book is available at quantity discounts for bulk purchases.
For information, please call 1-800-289-0963.*

Contents

Acknowledgments

JILL KONRATH for being my Diamond muse and inspiring me to new heights.

JILL ALEXANDER for being my Club editor and offering me expert advice.

JOHN WILLIG for being my Heart Agent and connecting me to the best people.

GWEN THOMAS, CHERYL GRADY, RITA WEBSTER, and LYNN SCHLEETER for their work as superior Spade implementors.

This book is the product of a lifetime of work with leaders and teams. The concepts in *Play Your Best Hand* started forming seven years ago when I led an informal Friday 7:30 A.M. workshop for a few people on the topic, "How to Discover Your Talents." To our amazement, over 425 people registered! At every level in the company, individuals wanted to know how to use their talents better. We moved the session out of the small conference room into the main auditorium and I've been working with leaders and talents ever since.

With such demand, I asked myself, *"How can I make it easy for individuals to bring their best talents to the business?"* Soon, I was buzzing with ideas.

First I designed Play to Your Strengths Talent system decks to help leaders and team members recognize and use each other's talents. Many individuals encouraged me along the way. I'm indebted to Stephanie McGovern, who helped me design the first Play to Your Strengths training sessions and connected me with valuable resources and interested clients. Thank you Stephanie!

Ralph Colby is the unsung hero in my business. With his Club assistance, I was able to design a workable train-the-trainer program and set up a viable business model. Ralph's creative genius on the topic of trust also helped me make the connection between talent types and trust issues. Thank you Ralph!

In the arena of consultants and clients, I want to thank Rita Webster from Wise Leader Inc., Gwen Thomas from East Central Energy, Cheryl Grady from BlueCross BlueShield of Minnesota, Lynn Schleeter from the Center for Sales Innovation at the College of St. Catherine, Marci Heerman from my Awesome Women's group, and Mike Evers, former dean and professor from the Graduate School of Business at the University of St. Thomas. These leaders were the original pioneers who implemented these ideas. Gwen Thomas's solid commitment to creating a customer-focused organization was the first real test of this concept. Cheryl Grady's no-nonsense approach to change management made these ideas come alive. And the patient and persistent commitment of Rita Webster as a certified consultant has paved the way for many clients to succeed using this approach. Lynn Schleeter threw her hat into the ring early and was the first person to introduce the talent types into the sales arena. I'm also indebted to my son Andrew Ralston who helped me develop our amazing Web-based technology for Play to Your Strengths Talent Assessments. And for saving my sanity throughout, I want to applaud Chris Bedwell, my virtual administrative assistant who has been a rock of support as we tested, retested, and revised the system until it was right. Thank you Chris for watching out for my backside.

To you all—I realize that without your ideas and support, none of this would have made it off my computer and into the world. I am truly grateful for your encouragement, belief in this approach, and your personal support. Thank you from the bottom of my heart!

INNOVATORS   MOTIVATORS   ACTIVATORS   IMPLEMENTORS

Part 1

Learn the New Game

Chapter 1

Lead the Wild Card— Managing Knowledge Workers

GETTING THINGS DONE IS important. Really important! As a leader, you're under constant pressure to achieve business goals in less time with fewer resources. You have employees to manage—as well as a full plate of your own. Whether you have 3 or 300 individuals reporting to you, they all want your time. And time is the one thing you don't have! You've got to do more with less—and maximizing talent is the most effective way to do it.

Customers Want More

Welcome to the new economy. Hierarchy, silos, and order, so essential to the industrial world, are now the enemies of speed and innovation. Successful innovation from idea generation to execution drives such products as the iPod into the marketplace. Customers' demand for new products, competitive pricing, shorter time to market, plus more partners in the collaborative mix means that you and your staff have four times the work and less time to do it.

3

Leaders Want More

As a leader, you dream of having talented employees. You want engaged and committed workers. You've seen the power of individuals collaborating and making things happen. But too often it's not that way. Your time is squandered on turf issues, poor performance, and projects that run over time and budget.

So you fantasize about starting with a blank slate, hiring a new group of employees, cloning the high performers, and someday becoming agile and results-oriented like the entrepreneurial companies your see in the marketplace.

Employees Want More

Employees also dream of doing great and wonderful things. What motivates and excites employees is the opportunity to develop their skills, learn from others, and tackle new endeavors. For many it's stressful and disheartening to deliver less than their best. Some employees are dedicated and driven—often working fifty to sixty hours a week. Yet these same employees confide to their friends, "I'm frustrated with my job. There's so much more I could do for this organization. If only I could find a way."

So employees fantasize. They dream about leaving and starting their own business, writing a book, becoming a consultant, and finding a place where they will be appreciated and given the opportunity to do meaningful work.

Ironically, the goals of employees and leaders have never been more aligned. Leaders want high performance, innovative solutions, and fast results. And employees want to use their talents and contribute in meaningful ways.

Yet according to the latest studies, most leaders are not even close to realizing employees' full potential. A recent Conference Board survey reported that a whopping 66 percent of employees do not feel highly motivated to drive their employer's business goals—and 25 percent say they are just showing up for a paycheck. If taken to heart, this means the average knowledge worker is contributing only 50 percent of what they are capable of delivering.

Whether these individuals leave their position in six weeks, six months, or six years, they've already checked out mentally. And the company's performance reflects their lackluster commitment.

The New Game of Business

The workplace is radically different than it was even ten years ago. To capture the talents and potential of today's work force, leaders must recognize the dramatic rise in the number of knowledge workers and the implications of this change. In a high-growth business, up to 50 percent of employees might be knowledge workers.

What's a Knowledge Worker?

Management guru Peter Drucker described knowledge workers as individuals who use knowledge, theories, and concepts, rather than physical labor, to complete work tasks. Knowledge workers are the individual contributors and professional managers who work as financial analysts, information specialists, planners, researchers, legal and human resources personnel, software designers, health care professionals, and social service employees in your business—just to name a few. Their talents are measured in the quality of their ideas and the value they contribute to a company's products, services, and processes.

Knowledge Workers Fuel Economic Growth

Knowledge workers are the fuel that fire economic growth. Smart knowledge workers offer a competitive advantage.

Through their ingenuity and creativity, knowledge workers create new products and services, shrink cycle times, re-engineer outdated processes, solve customer problems, implement strategic initiatives, develop software solutions, and offer expert advice.

Knowledge workers are no longer "cogs" in your business but virtual wheels of information and peer networks that drive the success of new initiatives. The speed at which these employees maximize and leverage their collective talents directly impacts your bottom line.

Knowledge workers enjoy working on productive teams and interacting with bosses and colleagues who inspire them to new heights. Essentially, knowledge workers want nothing more than to see their talents take your business to the top!

Knowledge Workers Are the Wild Card

In the end, it's the hearts and minds of knowledge workers that ensure business success. Knowledge workers are the "wild card" in business today. By definition, a wild card is the card that completes your hand. These talented individuals want to help you create the vision; they want abundant opportunities to develop their talents and make things happen. Your job as a leader is to help them succeed.

The challenge is that knowledge workers do not respond to traditional management practices. They are independent, often ego-driven, and chafe at micromanaging or corporate bureaucracy. Some days you may wonder if they even need you at all! However, without effective leadership, knowledge workers can spin off on tangents, make costly decisions, and waste valuable time and resources.

For the first time in organizational history, knowledge workers have the ball in their court. They can leave or they can stay.

They can offer their best—or just get by with the minimum. Your role is to help employees grab the ball and run with it. But taking hold is difficult. In today's chaotic environment, roles and responsibilities are fuzzy and decision-making is complicated. The real business needs exist in the white spaces between departments and organizational lines. With limited time and scant resources at your disposal, how do you help knowledge workers take charge and get things done? And how do you ensure high performance and results?

A New Approach to Leadership

Leading knowledge workers requires a new approach. To access 100 percent of knowledge workers' talents, you must help individuals leverage their strengths. Focusing on strengths—rather than deficiencies—helps knowledge workers make powerful contributions. Knowledge workers want to develop their skills—and they don't respond well to criticism and nitpicking. They're more talented and educated than the workers of previous decades—and thus, more independent and ego-driven. Micromanaging their projects and mistakes will quickly deflate their initiative. You still need to address problems and deficiencies, but not at the expense of asking, "How can we build on your strengths? Where can you best contribute?" All the time and attention currently being spent on employee weaknesses is as effective in today's fast-paced economy as a buggy whip on high-tech automobiles.

Focusing on Strengths Yields Benefits

Contradicting years of management training and methodology, leaders who adopt a strengths-based approach are able to increase productivity, lower costs, and accelerate business results. A strengths focus helps knowledge workers discover their hidden talents, recognize blind spots, compensate for weaknesses, and contribute greater value.

Focusing on strengths helps knowledge workers:

- Recognize and contribute their best talents.
- Take initiative and accept responsibility for results.
- Mix and match talents to meet changing requirements.

A strengths focus also helps leaders:

- Transform C players into A players.
- Retain talented employees.
- Do more with fewer resources.

Play Your Best Hand is a practical guide to help you get more done with the resources you have. The skills and ideas in this book are ideal for leaders of knowledge workers. This is a practical how-to book, full of insights and approaches you can immediately use to improve individual and team performance. The tools and solutions provided are based on thirty years of successful experience working with thousands of leaders and teams across a broad range of businesses.

By adopting the principles in this book, you'll rapidly empower employees to take charge and make their best contribution. You'll learn the inside scoop about what knowledge workers want from you, how to address performance issues, build greater trust among individuals, and turn more responsibility over to employees.

Most importantly, you'll learn how to help employees deliver what matters most to your customers. This book offers a fresh, new approach for leading and motivating knowledge workers to achieve results.

Getting Started

To embrace this strengths-based leadership style, you'll need to break old habits and challenge your current leadership practices. You'll discover that helping knowledge workers bring their best to the business means leading with *your* strengths. You focus on talents and talk openly about what's working and what's not. *Play Your Best Hand* helps you utilize the talents that already exist in your organization and build a positive work culture. This 180-degree shift in mindset and approach is just what you and employees need to thrive in the twenty-first century. Learn how to lead the "wild card"—and win.

KEY HIGHLIGHTS OF CHAPTER 1

- In the past thirty years traditional management practices have turned on their ear. We are rapidly transitioning from a manufacturing to a knowledge-based economy.

- The new economy is now fueled by the creative talents of knowledge workers. Knowledge workers use their brains instead of brawn to make a living.

- Knowledge workers are the "wild card" in business today. Their commitment, or lack thereof, can make or break your organization.

- All the time and attention currently being spent on employee weaknesses is as effective in today's fast-paced economy as using a buggy whip on a high-performance automobile.

- A strengths-based leadership approach taps the talents and potential of knowledge workers. Embrace this mindset by recognizing and leveraging your own talents.

Chapter 2

Are You In or Out of the Game?

TODAY IT'S A 24-7 global economy. Implementing projects requires greater collaboration and teamwork than ever before. Fortunately, knowledge workers thrive in this type of environment. They like figuring out solutions and tackling problems. Most of the time, they don't need to be given exact direction on how to address issues. As talented experts, they like to bring *their* expertise and experience to bear on complex problems.

Your role is to help employees see the big picture, be clear about the desired outcome, and navigate the political landscape so they can implement the changes needed. In essence, you must help knowledge workers take charge.

Employees Have a Choice

For the first time, employees have a choice about how they get work done. Information technology enables employees to find information and make informed decisions. But many don't feel free to lead. With downsizing, mergers, and outsourcing, they are hesitant to make decisions that threaten the status quo or their livelihood. So employees wait for others to decide—then feel disappointed when their views are not heard or acted upon.

In a presentation at a high-profile financial institution, I encouraged participants to talk about their talents and where they could add value to the organization. A woman in the back of the room raised her hand and said, "I am in a job that doesn't use my talents. But I'm sure my boss doesn't want to hear this. I'd never tell him what I could do for this organization." She felt helpless to bring her best talents to the table. Even more tragic is that she could not bring this up with her boss. She felt stuck in the old industrial mindset of waiting to be told what to do and stifled by a manager that didn't empower her to speak up.

It's Now a Take-Charge World

Your role as a leader is to help knowledge workers step up and take charge. You do this by encouraging employees to recognize their strengths, identify business priorities, and align their talents with these needs. Even with encouragement, many employees are hesitant to take charge fully—and sometimes leaders stand in their way. Many managers have not yet developed a comfort level with the attitudes and skills required to take charge. However, the old formula for success won't work in today's economy

Employees Must Think More Than Do

As we transition away from the industrial age, it's important to recognize that the outdated success formula from this era is what is hard-wired into our psyches. The formula for success in the factory was "Obey the rules." A factory could not survive if everyone "did their own thing" on the assembly line. This "Do what you're told" formula worked well for the industrial business model. But this same mindset does not foster the innovation and initiative required for success today.

Customer responsiveness and product innovation require more than obedience. Employees must take change and use their talents to add value. The key to success is not conformity—but initiative. Employees must grasp what's happening, see what's needed, and use their talents wisely to take initiative and add value.

Here's a brief summary of the old versus new behaviors you must foster to help employees thrive in today's economy:

OLD WAY	NEW WAY
Blend in	Speak up
Wait and see	Propose solutions
Tunnel vision	See the big picture
Task focus	Target outcomes
"It's not my job"	Take responsibility

Your job as a leader is to help knowledge workers see the big picture, understand the goals, contribute value, and use their talents to achieve meaningful results. Leaders must also transition to a new set of responsibilities and work priorities, and move from the old way of working to a new way:

FROM	TO
Manage a function	Ensure outcomes
Supervise employees	Orchestrate teamwork
Be the expert	Find the experts
Make decisions	Gain commitment to decisions
Know the answers	Coach others to find the answer

The Seven Deadly Sins of Leading Knowledge Workers

To successfully lead knowledge workers you must avoid the following ways of doing business.

Number 1: Focusing Only on What's Wrong

Too many leaders adopt a "no news is good news" approach to managing their staff. If an employee isn't screwing up, the manager basically leaves them alone. But knowledge workers want to be recognized. Positive encouragement highlights their talents, helps them continue moving in the right direction, and fuels their enthusiasm to offer more. Avoid focusing only on what's wrong, and acknowledge what's going right.

Number 2: Ignoring Poor Performers

High-performing knowledge workers expect you to deal with poor performers—otherwise the problem lands in their laps. You may have to reassign an individual to an area where their talents are better suited—or re-evaluate their position in the organization altogether. In either case it means paying attention to the problems and taking corrective action. Don't let a poor performer derail the progress and motivation of other employees.

Number 3: Neglecting Employees

Knowledge workers need your time and attention. They don't need a lot of it but they definitely need some. In today's busy workplace, leaders can go for weeks without checking in or talking with employees about how they are doing. You may not feel the need to communicate if you know projects are on track—but employees definitely need to connect. Regular check-ins and one-on-one meetings with employees keep knowledge workers motivated and momentum strong. Make sure you spend adequate time with each individual.

Number 4: Overlooking Boredom and Talent Misfit

Job uncertainty and fear of change may prevent employees from speaking up about a change that's needed. It's your job to notice when individuals start losing interest, are struggling in their current position, or are slacking off. We know from research that the longer employees stay in the same job, the less energy and motivation they have for the position. Maintaining high performance requires shaking things up. Address these issues head-on instead of letting them linger. Most knowledge workers don't get any satisfaction in just getting by. You do no one a service by allowing a bad fit to continue. Tough love with self and others is part of moving into the new economy.

Number 5: Failing to Give Useful Feedback

In corporate life, no one wants to hear, "This isn't working." However, employees need feedback. No matter how exceptional the individual, there are times when he might shoot himself in the foot without knowing it. A wise leader helps knowledge workers see problems and address the issues. Ideally you don't wait until there is a crisis to raise a touchy subject and give feedback.

Number 6: Saying "Yes" to Everything

Help knowledge workers curb their appetite to work on interesting projects that are unrelated to business priorities. No matter how exciting a project is, you must encourage knowledge workers to ask, "Is this project contributing to the primary goals of the business? Can I justify the time and energy I'm spending on it? Will this initiative, new project, strategic initiative, or R&D effort produce the outcomes we want?" Many times, knowledge workers will bite off more than they can chew. A wise leader helps employees set limits and say no—for their own sake as well as the sake of the business. They encourage employees to ask the tough questions and take a stand so valuable resources aren't wasted.

Number 7: Keeping Employees in the Dark

Knowledge workers need information to be effective. Good communication about strategic priorities and political realities helps them contribute in meaningful ways. With this knowledge they can make better decisions, involve the right people, avoid missteps, and move in the right direction. Without this essential information, they waste valuable time and resources on projects that are irrelevant. Nothing annoys a knowledge worker more than wasting time on meaningless activities. It's your job to keep knowledge workers in the communication loop so they can make good decisions about their time.

What Knowledge Workers Really Want

Your primary role is to help knowledge workers make a difference. To do so, you must understand knowledge workers and what makes them tick. Achieving this goal requires learning about knowledge workers and what motivates them. The following identifies what knowledge workers want you to know about them.

Give Them the Ball

Knowledge workers don't want to be told what to do. Rather, they want to be asked for their opinions, and they want to be given responsibility to achieve specific goals. Once knowledge workers know the desired outcomes you want for a project, they want the freedom to make decisions, develop a plan of action, and figure out how to move forward. They are willing to do small tasks if they relate to a larger project. But when you ask these individuals to complete minor tasks without knowing why, they perceive it as grunt work. Basically, the more autonomy you can extend knowledge workers to achieve their goals, the more willing they are to be involved and get results.

Let Them Do It Their Way

Too much direction and advice is insulting to knowledge workers. These employees have their own way of tackling projects and getting results. Knowledge workers don't want you to impose your way of doing things on them. They have a pattern and rhythm that works for them and they want to use it. Allow them to complete projects in their own way, as long as they accomplish the objective and don't interfere with other employees or processes.

Respect Their Input and Ideas

Nothing annoys a knowledge worker more than being overlooked in areas where they have expertise. They are insulted when you do not consult them on decisions in areas in which they can offer expert advice—even if it falls outside the strict parameters of their job. The developer wants to be included when her prototype is being reviewed, while a project manager wants to have a say in how his project is modified. Take time to involve knowledge workers in key decisions and welcome their input.

Give Them Time to Think

Thinking is the knowledge worker's stock and trade. These employees need both time and space to think about new ideas and make plans for the future. Time away from the office and away from the pressure of daily activities and immediate demands is essential. Knowledge workers want time to explore and consider new ideas without having to account for every minute they spend in and out of the office. Allow individuals to plan their schedule with some flexibility and have time away from the office.

Help Them Deal with Conflicts

Knowledge workers do not like getting mired in turf issues and destructive interpersonal dynamics. Many are not adept at handling conflicts and political infighting—they see it as a petty distraction to the work that needs to get done. Thus, they prefer to work around, ignore, and avoid dealing with conflicts and difficult personalities that impede progress. Yet, sometimes the problems caused by these disruptions are too great to ignore. Knowledge workers need your help confronting difficult issues and addressing them. As a leader of knowledge workers, you must get involved, help them confront tough issues, and make sure problems are resolved.

Encourage Them to Grow
Knowledge workers love to develop new talents and abilities. They relish learning, collaborating with colleagues, and stretching their minds and capabilities. Opportunities to grow and develop are enticing and motivate them to stay. Ideally you will provide many learning and development opportunities.

Set Them Up for Success
Knowledge workers don't like to be out of the communication loop or away from the action. They want to work on meaningful, high-impact projects. Just using their talents isn't enough. They want to feel that their work makes a difference—in the company, the industry, or the world at large. You must help knowledge workers align their talents with the real needs of the business. These employees know that getting sidetracked on low-priority or low-visibility projects is a waste of time. Ideally, you will help employees source work opportunities related to their interests and talents that are aligned with business needs.

Keep Them Well Informed
As a leader you have a wide-angle view of the organization. Your job is to share the broader vision. You see what priorities

are important. Make sure to communicate these priorities to employees. You need to convey the big picture and tell employees what's going on. This empowers them to make decisions that are aligned with the business and ensure their work has meaning in the organization.

Get in the Game

Letting go of the traditional ways of managing isn't easy. Remnants of the Industrial Age will linger as part of the culture for a long while. In the music industry, many executives still want to stamp, label, package, and ship CDs—even though music lovers prefer to download individual selections onto their iPods. An entire industry is trying to hang on for dear life, even as the market radically shifts around them. Your role is to help employees understand these shifts and take charge. Knowledge workers respect leaders who help them grow and address challenges. They want to work for strong, vibrant leaders. The question is, "Do you want *to be in or out of this new game?*"

KEY HIGHLIGHTS OF CHAPTER 2

- The new game in business is all about making a difference.
- Your role as a leader is to help knowledge workers make their best contribution.
- Employees now have a choice about the quality of work they do and who they will do it for.
- Helping employees use their talents is key to motivating, recruiting, and retaining knowledge workers.
- Knowledge workers want to work for a leader they respect.

Chapter 3

Learn the Rules

TODAY'S CORPORATE MANDATE is "Do more with less." Thus with more work and smaller budgets, leaders are asking "How can I optimize my current resources?" The truth is, there are more resources available than you think. Often the resource shortage exists because too many individuals are using a "Go it alone" approach. You can't leverage available resources without maximizing individual talents.

We're in This Together

The lone ranger or "go it alone" mindset is another leftover from the industrial age. To access 100 percent of employee talents, you need to help employees develop a collaborative mindset. Knowledge workers know the value of relationships and professional networks. Many routinely work in team settings and matrix environments. Yet, despite being in meetings all day, few are taking full advantage of the talents that surround them.

Accessing each other's talents demands greater collaboration than we're used to. We may be spending more time together in meetings, but we're still working separately, often to our detriment.

Over the past thirty years, I've worked with leaders and teams to help them implement their vision. Despite differences, many of these leaders faced a similar challenge. They all saw the need for greater teamwork and synergy to achieve their vision. To help them succeed, I developed the Play to Your Strengths Talent System. This approach provides a road map for leaders who want to improve team performance and optimize individual talents.

In this chapter, you'll learn the basics rules of this model. In later chapters you'll gain tools and methodologies to help you put the model into action. The ultimate goal of this approach is to help the employees on your team, and in your organization, take charge of their talents and make their best contribution.

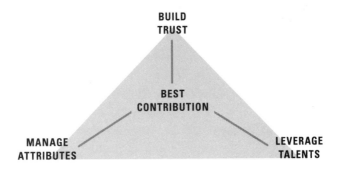

Rule Number 1:
Leverage Individual and Team Talents

To help employees contribute their best, begin by focusing on their talents. If you have a "C-player" in a particular position, you typically have three options.

1. Continue to allow that person or function to operate at 50 percent efficiency.
2. Hire more people to make up for the C-player's lack of talent.
3. Spend considerable time and money trying to develop the C-player for a role that individual may not have the natural talent for anyway.

None of these options helps your organization or the persons involved to be more competitive.

Ensure Talent and Job Fit

Achieving high performance requires insights into employee talents and making a deliberate effort to ensure job fit. Between 70 and 80 percent of an individual's job should be aligned with his or her natural talents. As the leader, you cannot leave talent utilization to chance. You must help employees discover their talents and recognize where they support business needs.

Talent Is Innate

Talents are different than a person's functional expertise. An employee might be a specialist in marketing. But marketing is not their talent—it's their functional expertise. Talents are the employee's natural abilities and skill, rather than an acquired body of knowledge. One employee may be naturally creative, while another is innately thorough, and still another communicates with astonishing ease.

Employee talents show up as aptitudes or skills that they perform easily. Talents are what set employees apart and make them unique. For example, in a department filled with engineers, one may be visionary, while another likes to organize, and yet another excels at developing people. These engineers all have the same technical expertise but vastly different talents. As a leader of knowledge workers, you need to be a talent scout because oftentimes employees are blind to their talents. Why? Because their talents are so easy and natural for them that they don't see them or realize their value. Your job is to make talents visible so employees can use them intentionally.

Discover Employee Talents

To help employees discover their talents, invite them to talk about what they enjoy doing. Encourage them to reflect on what they choose to do when they have free time. Also ask employees if they have ever received a thank-you note, appreciative e-mail message, or a reference letter from clients. These words of praise, or even criticism, are grist for discovering their talent strengths. Ask them to look for recurring patterns, key words, and phrases. These can provide clues to what they do best.

Value Different Talents

Sometimes it's difficult to immediately see the value of an individual's unique talent. In a workshop, a project manager named Cheri described how she loved to talk with people in her organization and find out what was going on. She had a reputation for knowing all the rumors circulating in the company. Cheri was a virtual grapevine of informal news and information. Her colleagues nicknamed her "Scoop" because she always knew the latest gossip. Obviously, this was her talent. Her family and friends also saw her exercise this talent at home, in her neighborhood, and around town. She was a walking fountain of knowledge.

Initially, when we talked about her talent, Cheri was embarrassed and laughed it off as unimportant. She said, "It's just something I do." But as we talked she started to see the potential value of her "scoop" abilities. She realized she could harness this talent to help managers in her company lead change initiatives. Cheri turned her natural ability into a valuable contribution. She recognized how people felt and what they needed to commit to change. She saw potential roadblocks, potholes, and ways to get around them. Over time Cheri became a valuable resource as she advised her manager about employee concerns and helped her manager develop strategies to engage people. With Cheri's help, her manager was able to communicate the right messages and gain employee commitment to changes and initiatives.

No two individuals on your team have exactly the same talents. Encourage employees to recognize and discover the value of their unique talents.

Rule Number 2:
Manage Personal Attributes

Once employees know their talents, the next step is to help them recognize and manage personal attributes. Attributes describe an individual's style or way of relating to others. Employee attributes are different from their talents. A software engineer in a midsize technology firm might be a great designer, planner, or visionary. These are his talents. But his attributes are how he comes across to others. The employee might be seen as shy, vibrant, calm, energetic, determined, or persistent.

How employees are perceived is critical to their success. Knowledge work is complex and requires a great deal of interaction and communication with others. To get things done, knowledge workers must influence, collaborate, and advise others. The employee who is "abrasive" will not be as effective as the employee who is seen as easy to work with. Knowledge workers often lose sight of that reality. They often think that their great ideas, education, or skills will (and should) outweigh any eccentricities or social shortcomings. However, in the business world, clients and customers will tolerate negative attributes for only so long. I once read a book called *What You Think of Me Is None of My Business*, by Terry Cole-Whittaker. Unfortunately, what others think of us *is* important, because it impacts performance. Others' perceptions affect the individual's ability to influence and advise others—the stock and trade of a knowledge worker's profession. As a manager, you need to help knowledge workers understand that how they're perceived is important.

Attributes Enhance or Diminish Performance
Personal attributes can support or diminish the knowledge worker's contribution. For instance, Brian is a project manager. His talents are planning and managing project details. His personal attributes are "calm and easygoing." In essence, Brian is a calm, easygoing (his attributes) planner (his talent). Ideally, Brian is aware of the value he brings as a calm and easygoing planner. With his relaxed personality, Brian doesn't get bent out of shape when projects go sideways. This is the positive side of his easygoing nature.

But our best attributes can also be a liability. In another setting, Brian's easygoing style might be perceived as "lacking authority" or "weak." Brian may need to manage his laid-back nature and turn it up a notch to get the cooperation he needs to meet deadlines. Ideally, as his manager, you help Brian recognize when he must modify his easygoing style to ensure ongoing success.

Recognize Missing, Overused, and Undervalued Attributes
Attributes must be managed. Overused, underused, and missing attributes can cause problems for employees. In a research

and development team I worked with, the manager hired a talented, well-known expert named Randy. Randy was justifiably confident in his knowledge and expertise. He had credentials as long as his arm. But soon team members started to see the flip side of his confidence—arrogance. His arrogant attitude embarrassed the team and annoyed other departments. Even though Randy was a very talented researcher, his arrogance diminished his value and hurt the team.

On the positive side, someone who is a skilled technical expert and possesses "encouraging and collaborative" attributes will draw people like a magnet. This employee helps others and does what it takes to find solutions. In the age of constant technical change, the demand for collaborative attributes is high. Most organizations want technical experts who work smoothly with customers and nontechnical staff. Just remember attributes can be an asset or a liability given the particular situation.

Rule Number 3:
Build Trust with Others

The third rule of success is to help employees build trust with others. The level of trust your employees have with each other directly impacts their ability to contribute. The higher the trust level, the more others are willing to rely on their services and expertise. Trust also affects the degree to which others support an employee's projects and ideas. Without trust, the employee may not get a seat at the table. Others will find ways to meet their goals and avoid interactions of real importance.

As the leader, you must sound the alarm when trust issues are in the way of performance. If others are hesitant to work with a member of your team because there is low trust—it's time to get involved. Lack of trust is costly and difficult to ignore. The best strategy is to build trust early, before it's needed.

Rule Number 4:
Seek Feedback from the Customer

The fourth rule of success is to ask the customer about the value of your contribution. Fair or not, in today's marketplace, the customer decides whether your efforts have made their life better or worse, easier or more difficult. Knowledge workers may think they are doing a wonderful job, but the customer has the final say about their contribution.

Knowledge workers take pride in their work and strive to offer excellent service. However, the customer may not see their services as useful. It's difficult for any of us to realize we don't always meet our customer's expectations. In polls and surveys, 48 percent of employees rate themselves in the top 10 percent in their industry. Obviously, 48 percent can't be in the top 10 percent. Conversely, only a few employees rate themselves as doing poorly. Without feedback to the contrary, it's easy to assume we are delivering great value. You can help employees focus on the customer by encouraging them to:

- Learn upfront what others want to receive and how they want to be treated.
- Deliver the desired service or product in a way that exceeds expectations.
- Ask for feedback about the service and also about the customer's experience of working with you.
- Encourage employees to listen and adapt to changing customer expectations. Remind employees that their peers, internal customers, and others have valuable opinions they will not share unless they are directly asked for feedback.

Knowledge workers have a lot of pride in their abilities. To succeed, employees must shrink their ego and realize it's the customer who decides the value of their contribution. New ideas and research and development are great, but if they don't lead to tangible services and products your company can profit from, they're meaningless. As a leader, you can encourage employees to see feedback as a necessary reality check that improves their odds at winning.

In essence, knowledge workers want to succeed. And you can help them. Encourage them to discover and leverage their talents, recognize personal attributes, build trust with others—and most importantly—stay in touch with customers.

KEY HIGHLIGHTS OF CHAPTER 3

- You and your employees must let go of a "Do it myself" mindset to begin leveraging your collective talents.

- The easiest, fastest way to help employees contribute high value is to discover and leverage their talents.

- Our natural attributes—or style—can both help and hinder our success. Help employees manage personal attributes to ensure high performance.

- The degree of trust employees have with others directly affects their ability to contribute. Help employees build trust with one another.

- The customer decides the value of our contribution. Customer feedback is a gift that helps knowledge workers contribute their best.

Chapter 4

How to Play

YOU'VE SIGNED UP for the new game. Now how do you play it? You start by recognizing your talents as a leader. Perhaps, like me, you stumbled onto your talents early in life but didn't realize their value.

As a child, I didn't like school. In elementary school, my grades were below average. Unable to read until fourth grade, I thought I was dumb. My parents were so concerned they put me in a private school in fifth grade. In this environment, my performance improved and came up to grade level.

Midyear, my teacher, Mr. Holly, scheduled a parent-student conference. The purpose of the conference was to discuss the results of my standardized tests. Mr. Holly pointed at a graph that ran flat-line at the sixth-grade level until he reached "reading comprehension." Suddenly the graph flew off the page. I tested at the twelfth-grade level! That was the first time I had any inkling there was something I did exceptionally well.

Soon the test score was forgotten and I plugged along in school, mainly receiving C's. My high school guidance counselor told me I was not college material and advised me to enroll in a vocational school. Luckily, I ignored her advice and found a college that would take an average student.

In college, I worked hard. While the other students made good grades with ease, I plugged away. Despite my hard work, I still graduated with only a C+ average. Following graduation, I became an elementary teacher. I liked education but found the classroom confining. So I decided to become a guidance counselor.

But this meant graduate school. Now I had to find a university that would accept me into their graduate school program. Again I was discouraged by the admission counselor who told me my grades did not qualify me for advanced study. Finally I asked the counselor if I could take two trial courses and see how well I did. In these classes, I worked hard and managed to get a B+ in Statistics and an A+ in Introductory Psychology. The school agreed to let me enter their graduate program in counseling psychology.

From that point on, I soared all the way through graduate school and earned a master's degree and later a Ph.D. For the first time in my life, school was easy. I loved it and maintained a solid 4.0 average.

At my wedding, an invited professor told my father I was one of the most exceptional students the school had seen. His feedback shocked me. I hadn't worked that hard. And I never thought of myself as "smart." Yet my studies were relatively easy and I was making straight A's. What happened? I had discovered a subject area that intrigued me and that I was naturally good at learning. I had stumbled upon my talent.

Focusing on Talents Brings Success

I've built a career by leveraging the talents that come easily and naturally to me. Like me, you and your employees have natural talents and skills. Individuals typically have five to seven core talents they are good at using and one talent they especially love. As a leader, you want to recognize these natural talents and put them to work. When you access talents, several things will happen.

- Work is easier and more fun.
- Teamwork is less stressful and more productive.
- Employees are energized and excited about their jobs.
- Others show greater appreciation for the services they receive.

In counseling leaders on how to create high-performing teams, I've discovered the quickest way to improve performance and results is to free people up to do what they do best. Focusing on talents is the magic bullet for improving performance.

The Play-to-Your-Strengths Principles

Business is about getting things done. And it's easier to get things done when your work is aligned with your talents. As a leader, you want to help employees discover their talents and fully use these abilities to address business needs. You want highly motivated employees who not only accept work assignments but also recommend projects that they can lead. Ultimately, you want employees who take charge of using their talents in a productive way. Your job is to help them take hold of their talents and expand the contribution they can make.

The Play to Your Strengths principles are the underpinning of this strengths-based leadership approach.

Principle Number 1: *Recognize That Every Person Has Unique Strengths*

Each individual on your team has a unique set of strengths. When you tap into these strengths, you're able to improve effectiveness and results. You also increase the energy and enthusiasm of employees. At one time or another, we've all experienced the rush of energy that comes from working on a project that plays to our strengths. We may stay late at work and get too little sleep at night, but our energy level still remains high. Put simply, when a project captures our interests, we have energy to spare.

But when we're working on a project that bores us, we watch the clock all day long. And we don't feel as though our skills are being used to the best advantage. When there's a mismatch between what we love to do and what we've been assigned, all the sleep, nutritious foods, vitamins, and exercise in the world won't stave off our low energy. We have to fight just to make it through the day. It's draining and unproductive for employees to be disconnected from their talents.

Boredom Signals the Need for Change

Boredom is a warning sign that we're not using our talents. This is especially true for knowledge workers. If you give them work that bores them, they are likely to become resentful and start looking for other opportunities. At the very least they'll work at a lower capacity. It's like driving an eight-cylinder car in first gear.

Focus on What's Right—Without Ignoring What's Wrong

Leveraging strengths is radically different from developing weaknesses. As a strengths-focused leader you pay more attention to what is going right than what is wrong. You *do* challenge mediocrity and confront performance issues. But you don't waste time trying to fix what you know you can't change. You refuse to waste time or money on development activities that go nowhere.

Principle Number 2: *We Are Often Blind to Our Strengths*

Our talents have been with us since birth. Talents are the skills we are naturally adept at doing. You'll always know when you've identified someone's talent correctly because they'll say, "Oh, it's easy," or "It's no big deal." Realize that when employees say, "It's no big deal," this is their talent showing up.

As a leader, it's important to let employees know when you see their talents in action. Without feedback employees are blind to their talents.

Principle Number 3: *Strive to Maximize Strengths— and Minimize Weaknesses*

Weaknesses are recognized in a strengths-focused organization. But leaders aim to minimize weaknesses—not fix them. Too many leaders have the notion that employees should be well rounded. Knowledge workers are typically not that well rounded. They are specialists in specific areas. Their talents come in all different shapes and sizes. The goal of developing employees is to leverage their strengths—rather than create a prototype of the ideal employee.

Stay Focused on Talents

Staying true to core talents is not always easy. When employees take on a new job, they're full of enthusiasm and look forward to the new challenge. But over time they inherit tasks that are not aligned with their talents and abilities. Without proactive attention to talents, employees can drift away from what they love. Expanding and growing in new areas is highly beneficial. But also recognize that the employees' core talents are home base. They need to continually come back to their core talents and use them as a springboard for growth. Staying grounded in core talents makes it easier for employees to learn new things, accept criticism, and address weaknesses. Help employees recognize their talents and stay true to these core abilities.

Principle Number 4: *Strengths Can Also Be Weaknesses*
All strengths have a flip side. Whenever you see an outstanding strength, also realize it can be trouble if overused. One employee might be a visionary, but clueless about immediate actions needed to achieve the vision. Another individual may have a talent for order and structure but have trouble being flexible and adaptable. The physician who excels in surgery may have trouble relating to hospital staff. One of your employees might be the social glue at your office, but inept at getting projects done. Discovering talents should be balanced by the recognition of their flip side.

Principle Number 5: *Seek Feedback to Leverage Strengths*
Too often, employees perceive that feedback is negative. Bear in mind that many employees have had a bad experience with feedback. One-on-one meetings and performance reviews are too often about tallying weaknesses rather than helping employees discover and develop their strengths. Managers are quick to share bad news and criticism. But when leaders assume that employees are doing well, they don't offer feedback.

In reality, employees actually need *more* feedback on what they are doing *right*. Remember, most employees are blind to their talents. Many are unaware of the positive impact they are having and the contribution they are making.

Feedback is a just-in-time development tool. It encourages behavior that works. Early feedback keeps knowledge workers on track and going in the right direction. Ideally, you make it easy for employees to give you feedback as well. You can invite feedback by asking, "What am I doing that is helpful to you in getting your job done/meeting company objectives? What could I do more of or less of to be effective as your supervisor?"

Feedback helps employees see the impact they are having in the organization. When they know what works, they can do it again, deliberately.

Address Weaknesses

Recognizing strengths makes it easier to address performance issues. You might have an individual like Jason. Jason wants everything he does to be perfect. Ideally, you praise Jason for his attention to detail and his commitment to excellence. But you also help him recognize when this attention to detail is getting in the way of working with others. Feedback helps Jason leverage his strengths and manage his weaknesses. Early feedback keeps Jason's Achilles' heel from becoming an Achilles' leg.

Encourage Strength Feedback

Encouraging strength feedback helps team members watch each other's backside. Feedback opens up communication about strengths and raises awareness of both strengths and weaknesses. It's a multiple-win approach. When the members of your team learn how to give strength feedback, teamwork and collaboration increase. Instead of employees throwing up their hands and saying, "I just can't work with Ted," they address their concerns in a constructive way. Team members recognize that for every weakness, there is also an underlying strength. Potential conflicts are minimized and addressed early on.

Take this quick assessment and see how well you are playing into your strengths at work. Once you've completed the assessment, invite your employees to take the assessment and discuss it with you. Circle the number that represents where you fall on the scale.

PLAY TO YOUR STRENGTHS TALENT ASSESSMENT

1. Do you know your best talents?

No	1	2	3	4	5	Yes

2. Do you routinely communicate your talents to others?

No	1	2	3	4	5	Yes

3. Do others perceive your talents the same way you do?

No	1	2	3	4	5	Yes

4. Can you articulate the value your talents bring to others?

No	1	2	3	4	5	Yes

5. Are you routinely doing work that requires your best talents?

No	1	2	3	4	5	Yes

What's Your Score?
20–25 means exceptional use of talents.
15–19 means you're making progress.
0–14 means you have more to offer.

Focusing on strengths enables employees to do what they do best and move key initiatives forward. Helping employees align their strongest talents with business needs is the key to success.

KEY HIGHLIGHTS FROM CHAPTER 4

- Business is about getting things done. To make progress, leaders must align employees' talents with business needs.
- Improve performance quickly by freeing people up to do what they do best.
- Every employee has a unique set of strengths. When leaders tap into these strengths, they accelerate projects and results.
- Feedback makes our talents visible and helps us manage over- and underused strengths.
- Ideally, we strive to maximize our strengths and minimize our weaknesses.

INNOVATORS   MOTIVATORS   ACTIVATORS   IMPLEMENTORS

Part 2

Maximize Employee Talents

Chapter 5

Discover the Four Talent Types

IT'S ESTIMATED THAT eight out of ten people in organizations are in jobs not ideally suited to their talents. This type of mismatch is disheartening for employees and hinders your ability to get things done.

Dwight started a medical device company that was wildly successful. The organization grew from five to fifty employees in the first year. After six years, the organization had quadrupled in size. Dwight should have been ecstatic. But he was miserable. Work simply wasn't fun anymore. He longed for the good old days when money was tight and he was calling on customers every day.

Though he was talented as an entrepreneur, managing a mature business was simply not his ideal.

It's important to help employees realize where their talents do—and don't—fit. The same employee can be superior in one job and dreadful in another. All projects and change initiatives require different talent types to implement them successfully from start to finish. One employee might be exceptional in the start-up phase of a project while another is better at tying up the loose ends. If the knowledge worker is in the wrong role, the project will suffer.

Efficiency Programs Miss the Mark

Process improvement and quality management initiatives help leaders streamline work processes and make them more efficient. But these programs do little to align employee talents with changing work requirements. Optimizing employee talents is an untapped opportunity that can help leaders radically improve performance.

As a manager you need to ask, "What talents does the project require? Who are the right people to lead the project at this stage?" As the leader, you need to give permission for different talents to take the lead in certain areas and during certain phases of the project. You must ensure that the right mix of talent types are on the team for effective execution of strategies.

The Four Distinct Talent Types

In my research with over 300 individuals, I've discovered four distinct talent types. Each of these four talent types is necessary and contributes to success in a unique and different way. For ease of use, I have named these talent types: *Diamond Talents*, *Heart Talents*, *Club Talents*, and *Spade Talents*. Our Talent Assessment reveals that individuals use a mixture of these four talents in their roles. However, most individuals have a favorite, or "preferred talent." And roughly 80 percent of the individuals who take the Talent Assessment indicate they are "low" or deficient in one of these four essential talents.

What's important to know is that very few individuals have an equal measure of capability in all four talents. Yet all four talent types are necessary to implement work projects and change initiatives successfully.

For leaders, this means that you need to recognize the four talent types and make sure projects have the right mix of talents to succeed. You need to ensure that the four talent types are represented or available to the team, and that their ideas are respected.

The more savvy knowledge workers are about when to leverage their talents and when to rely on others, the more likely projects and initiatives are to succeed. You can learn more about the Play to Your Strengths Talent Assessment by visiting my Web site at *www.playtoyourstrengths.com*. Our 360 Talent Assessment is ideal for leaders who want to assess their personal leadership strengths, as well as team member strengths.

Every Talent Type Has a Key Role to Play

The following model reveals how each talent type contributes to project success. At the beginning of a project, a Diamond Talent often initiates the project. The Diamond Talent comes up with new and innovative ideas. But, when the project is nearing completion, a Spade Talent is needed. The Spade Talent likes to manage the details and tie up loose ends.

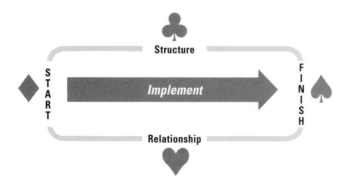

Overseeing the entire project is the Club Talent. The Club Talent likes to champion the idea and set up a structure that ensures success. Supporting it all is the Heart Talent. The Heart Talent makes sure employees are working well together and motivated to achieve the goals. All four of the talent types have a role to play at different times in the life cycle of a project. In each stage of a project, different talents must take the lead.

Summary of the Four Talent Types

The following is a summary of the four talent types. Notice how each talent contributes to project success in a different way.

Diamond Talents

Diamond Talents like to recognize emerging needs and imagine solutions. They are masters of possibility thinking. The Diamond Talent looks for options and comes up with out-of-the-box solutions. Diamonds look for "diamonds in the rough," or those ideas among many that hold hidden potential. Without Diamond Talents there's little creativity or innovation on the team.

Club Talents

Club Talents like to champion a good idea and set up structures that ensure its success. The Club Talent uses his or her personal and organizational power to transform ideas into reality. Without the structure and support offered by Club Talents, new ideas lack sufficient funding or resources—and they wither and die.

Spade Talents

Spade Talents like to organize what needs to be done and make sure projects are taken to completion. The Spade Talent literally "digs in" and gets things done. The Spade Talent orchestrates the details of implementation and makes sure projects are completed on time and within budget. Without Spade Talents, deadlines and details are frequently missed.

Heart Talents

Heart Talents like to motivate others, foster teamwork, and gain buy-in and commitment to new initiatives. Heart Talents often deal with "matters of the heart." Low morale, mistrust, and team conflicts require the soothing skills of Heart Talents. Without adequate Heart Talents, employee commitment and frustration can skyrocket.

Essentially, Diamond Talents provide the innovative spark that creates new products and services. Club Talents make it possible for new ideas to become a reality. Spade Talents make sure projects are completed and cross the finish line. And Heart Talents keep teamwork and relationships on track and humming. To succeed, projects and new initiatives need all four talents. By recognizing these different talent types, you can make sure you have the right talents in place to succeed with organizational initiatives.

As you read the descriptions of each type, think of an individual in your organization who fits the description. This will help you remember the qualities of each talent type for use later with your team.

Leverage Diamond Talents

Individuals with Diamond Talents like to think outside the box. They are good at spotting trends, creating innovative solutions, and generating ideas. They are expert problem solvers because they can see a problem from every angle. Diamond Talents like to think about what's possible. With their keen insights they perceive needs, revamp systems and processes, and suggest alternative solutions. Diamond Talents like to synthesize ideas, develop theories, research information, and design innovative solutions. A Diamond Talent often challenges the status quo.

The Diamond mind runs a mile a minute. They link ideas from unusual and unrelated sources. In conversations, they quickly jump from one thought to the next—and their statements may appear to have no connection to what others are talking about.

The Diamond's ideas seem to come out of the blue. If you are working with several Diamonds in a team meeting, they may brainstorm ideas that others can't follow. Diamond Talents are not bound by the realities of the current situation. They can see reality, but they're not constricted by it. Diamonds are more interested in what could potentially exist or be created than in the here and now. They invent solutions that others can't imagine.

Diamond Talent Strengths

Without Diamond Talents onboard, a team or an entire organization can miss windows of opportunity. Diamonds are the ones who ask, "What about this idea? Have you thought about trying that?" If a team has few Diamond Talents, the members may get stuck in the status quo and see limited options and solutions.

Diamond Talents like to:

- Create innovative solutions
- Challenge the status quo
- See issues and opportunities
- Think outside the box
- Envision a brighter future

The Diamond Intellect

Diamonds love a mental challenge. The Diamond Talent is perfect if your team is developing a new product or program. At the start of a project, Diamonds quickly generate innovative ideas, and then trudge through data and information to find the "jewel" that makes things work. Diamonds are frequently the geniuses behind new products and innovations that enter the marketplace.

Diamonds thrive on the stimulation of new ideas and possibilities. They like to start with a blank sheet of paper or a vague concept. Ambiguity and the unknown invigorate them. They are innovative and creative in this situation. Often, they are good at research because it stimulates their active minds. They love to come up with the big idea that has great potential.

Key Challenges for a Diamond Talent

The Diamond Talent often sees ideas and solutions before others even start to think about the problem. Diamonds are visionaries. They observe trends and see into the future. The problem is they don't take other people through their thinking process. Many times colleagues are confused and don't understand the value of the Diamond's idea until later. Frequently, Diamond Talents will have to wait for others on the team to catch up with their visionary ideas. Diamonds need to help others understand how they came to a conclusion. They also need to be careful not to send condescending vibes when others don't understand their ideas.

Diamond Talent Work Preferences

Diamonds enjoy consulting and advising with many diverse groups and individuals. They are proud of their expertise—and rightly so. They don't like to be stuck physically or mentally in one place. Too much of the same thing is boring and stagnating. Variety and novelty are what interests them. In a large organization the ideal scenario for a Diamond Talent is to serve as an expert advisor to a variety of individuals, teams, and projects. Diamonds want to be with others who stimulate their thinking. They like being involved in the start up of projects and to tackle challenging problems that arise throughout. But they do not want to get "stuck" with the day-to-day activities and demands.

Diamonds also want to be appreciated—not shunned for their thinking and out-of the-box solutions. They love to learn and grow. Diamonds will seek stimulating environments and outlets for their creative minds.

The Diamond-Type Organization

Sometimes entire organizations are dominated by Diamond Talents, particularly research and development firms. When you visit these firms it's not uncommon to encounter a lot of freewheeling, independent mavericks. Sandia National Labs in Albuquerque, New Mexico, typifies an organization dominated by Diamond Talent. In these labs there are hundreds of Ph.D.s scurrying around with all kinds of creative energy, working to develop new ideas and programs.

Apple Computer is another Diamond organization. The iPod is an out-of-the-box innovation of famed entrepreneur and inventor Steve Jobs. If you step inside the company headquarters, you experience the chaos that permeates this Diamond-intensive organization. Today, this Diamond organization is changing the marketplace and causing competitors to scramble.

How to Lead Diamond Talents

Getting Diamond Talents to line up and march in unison is difficult. These individuals see themselves as entrepreneurs working within a corporate environment. Diamond-dominated companies and teams benefit by partnering with the other talent types. They need Club Talents, who provide structure and ensure funding; Spade Talents, who help them complete what they start; and Heart Talents, who foster the collaboration necessary to implement their idea. Otherwise, a solely Diamond-driven team or organization can spin out of control with too many ideas and too little execution.

Maximize Club Talents

The Club Talent wants to launch new initiatives. Club Talents champion ideas, secure resources, build alliances, and initiate changes needed to bring a vision into reality. Individuals with Club Talents envision a brighter tomorrow and advocate for change. They often have a singular vision and clear purpose. Club Talents set up projects for long-term success.

Without Club Talents to champion ideas, strategic initiatives falter and good ideas die on the vine. An organization or team without Club Talents can falter for lack of a vision and purpose. Or there may be a vision, but without Club Talents, the systems, structures, and resources to support the vision will be lacking.

Club Talent Strengths

Clubs are the ones who say, "Let's do it," and "Let's do it right." The Club Talent likes to initiate change. They use their power to bring about significant change. Club Talents like to:

- Sponsor initiatives
- Advocate for change
- Build alliances and partnerships
- Put systems and resources in place
- Set up projects and initiate changes to achieve results

Club Talents are looking for an idea or a project that can grow and develop into something bigger. Once the Club Talent has a good idea, she or he locks onto it and doesn't let go. The Club launches into action and rallies the necessary people and resources to support the idea. Club Talents aren't interested in small, insignificant change. The Club needs to have a big vision to be enthusiastic about working on a project.

Club Talents exist at every level in the organization—and especially in leadership positions. Look for Club Talents in leadership positions and staff roles. They may be the formal or the informal lead, because they like to take charge.

A Club Talent scans the environment and sees what's missing. Unlike the Diamond Talent, who also looks for ideas, the Club settles in on one *big* idea and makes it happen. The Club Talent is gifted at creating structure. A Club may hang out with Diamonds to find a new idea or source new opportunities. Someone with a Club Talent quickly sees the value of an idea and does something about it. Transforming ideas into reality energizes the Club Talent. Club Talents are excellent at forging alliances both inside and outside the organization. Relationships are formed to support their vision. Clubs know what it takes to create lasting success. And despite the grandeur of their vision, they are not likely to get in over their head. Once the Club has a vision, he or she sits back and assesses what's needed to turn the idea into reality. Then the Club goes to work and systematically lays a solid foundation and puts the building blocks in place to support the vision.

Challenges for Club Talents

In the process of driving the vision, the Club Talent may ignore relationships unrelated to the vision. Conversely, they can also overvalue relationships that support their vision. In other words, Club Talents value individuals who bring resources and support to their vision but can overlook those who don't directly serve their goals. Because Clubs are so focused on achievement, they may overlook the emotional needs of others to be valued and appreciated. In their haste, they may not secure adequate buy-in from the people impacted by their ideas and what they're trying to achieve. Their intense focus on project success may turn off others seeking a more balanced approach to change. However, the Club Talent's systematic actions bring about impressive and sustainable change. The Club Talents may even distance themselves from individuals who are negative about their vision. Clubs need to learn how to stay open to negative feedback and not take it personally. Club Talents can gain greater buy-in and commitment by listening to Heart Talent colleagues. And they will benefit from the support of Spades who get things done.

Club Talent Work Preferences

Club Talent individuals want to move mountains. The bigger the mountain, the more energized the Club Talent feels. Club Talents do not like to maintain the status quo. They create something tangible and different. In leadership roles, Club Talents are involved in acquisitions, joint ventures, new product development, and product launches. Club Talent individuals exist at all levels of the organization. These individuals want to work on large projects of importance. In a leadership role, Club Talents find new ventures and companies to buy. As team leaders, they look for the next big strategic initiative to lead. Club Talents often work behind the scenes. They like to "work the deal" quietly and over time. Success, not power, is what matters.

The Club-Type Organization

Bill Gates is a perfect example of a Club Talent. He did not invent the Microsoft Operating System. Rather, he recognized the value of what a Diamond researcher had developed, brought the idea to market, and built the Microsoft organization from there.

MS-DOS proved to be a lucrative product, but the structure that Bill Gates put in place was critical to its success. A quarter of a century later, this structure is still intact. Microsoft is one of the most successful companies in the world; it has a huge share of its respective markets, consistently displays strong earnings, and shows little sign of slowing down. Bill Gates continues to use his Club talents to take Microsoft to the next level.

How to Lead Club Talents

Ask individuals who have strong Club Talents to work on projects that need development and require time to come to fruition. Expect Clubs to sell the idea, assemble the resources, and design the infrastructure to support this project. Tell them the outcome that you want and let them go to it. Be alert to success, because when the launch is done and the systems are in place, the Club Talent wants a new project. They quickly become bored and want a new challenge once the project is up and running. You may be surprised how fast they can walk away from what they have created once it's up and running smoothly. The Club Talent always needs a new challenge.

Clubs rarely get involved in doing the actual work that needs to be done. They set up structures where others actually do the work and tend to the details. Their forte is turning an idea into reality. They are the architects who set up the system so that the vision or project becomes real.

Energize Spade Talents

The Spade Talent likes to tackle projects and get them done. Spade Talents "dig in" and drive projects across the finish line. Spades like to take practical actions to move things forward. Spade Talents are the backbone of strategy execution. Individuals with Spade Talents often manage, run, and improve core processes and systems. They orchestrate both large and small actions needed to ensure progress. Spades remove barriers to performance, organize the work that needs to be done, and make sure all the i's are dotted and the t's are crossed.

With their persistent efforts and attention to details, Spade Talents manage the details and ensure results.

Essentially, Spade Talents like to:

- Complete projects
- Manage and improve processes
- Define and clarify actions needed
- Meet deadlines
- Handle the details

Spade Talents are outcome driven. They want to know goals, deadlines, and what's expected of them. Spades are task-oriented and dedicated. For Spades, reaching the goal is their raison d'être. While Diamond Talents like to conceive of new ideas, Spade Talents like to complete them.

Spades are "no-nonsense" individuals who loathe inefficiency. They are frustrated by delays and wasted effort. They dislike doing something twice when once should be sufficient. They like to have expectations in writing so the specifics are clear.

Challenges for the Spade Talent

Too many loose ends and chaos are disconcerting for Spades. Spades can become enmeshed in details and frustrated when problems don't get resolved. Often Spade Talents assume too much responsibility. They can get caught up in crises and too entwined in a project. Then they seek to control things even more and their efforts backfire or rub colleagues the wrong way. This frustrates Spades even further—they hate it when interpersonal glitches interfere with performance. They like to get things done and feel that relationship tensions are unnecessary distractions. Spade Talents may forget to back off and look at the big picture. Spades are focused on the immediate goals and what's essential to complete a project. They may not see the forest for the trees.

A Spade may continue to relentlessly pursue an initiative when it's time to pull the plug. A project design may have critical flaws that need to be reworked, but Spades take no time to regroup. They'll simply try to plow their way through and make things work. This can be exhausting for them and those who report to them.

Like Club Talents, they can overlook the human component and hence need Heart Talents to oil the interpersonal relationship gears. Spades need Diamond Talents to create new projects they can implement. Club Talents help Spade Talents remove barriers beyond their reach, while Heart Talents remind them to care about people as well as tasks.

Spade Talent Work Preferences

Spade Talents dislike starting from scratch. They find it easier to react to an idea or fill in a template. They prefer specifications and directions to a blank slate. If told to "go for it" they will ask for more directions and clarification. In a meeting where everyone is brainstorming ideas, a Spade Talent will try to nail down the specifics.

Spades want clarification and specifications from the leader. Often Spades will ask, "Who is doing what?" "What are the milestones?" "When is this due?" And "Let's get clear on what we are doing." To a Spade, good ideas are meaningless until such realities are addressed.

It's frustrating for a Spade Talent to sit in a meeting where a bevy of ideas are introduced. Until these ideas are given form and substance and put into a plan, Spade Talents consider it a waste of time.

Involve Spades more when the blue-sky brainstorming phase is over. For Spades, too much brainstorming and ideation are tedious. A Spade will say, "Just tell me what you want me to do." Spades love managing the details and making sure projects are on track. Give Spade Talents a clear goal and charter, clarify their role and your expectations of them, and they will make it happen.

Offer Spade Talents as much meaningful responsibility as you can. They love to work hard and do it well. Some Spades like to manage large projects. Others like to respond to immediate needs and requests. But all Spades love details and taking care of the fundamentals that keep projects moving in the right direction.

The Spade-Type Organization

Retail organizations are frequently dominated by Spade Talents. Nordstrom's and Macy's are wonderful examples of two value-driven Spade organizations. At the retail level, details and customer service are extremely important in these two Spade-driven organizations. Success is all about follow-through. The devil is in the detail. The sales personnel go out of their way to follow up, advise, find a replacement if needed, and ship products to customer's homes. Sales personnel are empowered but also given specific Spade-friendly guidelines to follow. In these stores, the extra time and attention customers receive in finding just the right item—with minimum hassle—is an example of a Spade organization in action.

Spade Talents are found at every level in the organization. Spade executives have a distinctive leadership style. The Spade executive or manager does not engage in idle chitchat or go to perfunctory meetings that lead nowhere. These individuals want agendas and documented progress reports. They are detail and results oriented. On projects, they often want staff to submit a written summary with a detailed follow-up plan. They will leave no stone unturned or detail untended to get the results they want.

How to Lead Spade Talents

Spade Talents want clear direction and the authority to do what the project requires. Once a Spade starts a project, he or she brings considerable energy to it. Throughout the project, Spade Talents want direction and input on the overall plan. With clear structure and goals, the Spade Talent can shine. When there is no clarity and direction, they'll work to create it. Expect Spade Talents to ask the tough questions that no one else brings to the table. Invite Spades to anticipate and head off issues before they happen. And don't be put off by the Spades' ability to see what's wrong and recognize potential pitfalls that might hinder the project. Listen and respect their concerns and you'll prevent problems later. Make it a point to recognize their hard work and acknowledge their heroic efforts to complete projects on time and within budget.

Value Heart Talents

The fourth talent that's critical to project success is the Heart Talent. Heart Talents are the invisible glue that makes projects and work relationships successful. Ironically enough, the Heart Talent is noticed most when it's missing rather than when it is present. Heart Talents keep relationships vital, team spirit high, and commitment strong. If your team or department is lacking these qualities, enlist a Heart Talent individual to help you.

Recognizing Heart Talents

Heart Talent individuals pay special attention to teamwork and employee morale. They are attuned to the needs and concerns of others. Heart Talents have a keen ability to sense people's needs and use their persuasive skills to get to the heart of the matter. They are experts at listening, coaching, communicating, and facilitating. Heart Talents like to connect, communicate, and inspire others to do their best.

This talent type is highly intuitive and sensitive to other people's emotions. They know when relationships are tense and headed toward conflict. They are excellent communicators and like to build trust and foster high morale.

Heart Talents excel at developing others' talents and expressing appreciation.

Heart Talents like to:

- Gain commitment
- Build trust and teamwork
- Resolve conflicts
- Listen and advise
- Influence others

Without Heart Talents, morale and trust levels can drop to an all-time low. The Heart Talent realizes that lack of motivation and poor teamwork delay project implementation. High turnover, mistrust, and turf wars indicate that Heart Talents are missing.

Heart Talent Strengths

Heart Talents build and promote successful relationships. They are sensitive to organizational dynamics and interpersonal tensions. Hearts help others understand why a decision or change is needed. They infuse others with positive enthusiasm and energy. They also promote the buy-in and commitment so essential for success.

A Heart Talent has many allies, friends, and acquaintances. Heart Talents like to connect, so they are out and about interacting and observing what's going on. They are often seen talking, persuading, motivating, and inspiring others.

Heart Talents enjoy lively meetings with colleagues who are connecting in meaningful ways. Heart Talents can sense lack of commitment on the part of others. They're attuned to those who are at or near burnout. They hear and sense when there is tension in the air. During meetings, they ask key questions that surface underlying tensions. All the while, they strive to bring harmony and clarity to the group.

Challenges for Heart Talents

Heart Talents can assume too much responsibility for the burdens of others. They feel all the dynamics going on among team members. Others frequently come to them with their problems and concerns. Heart types can become overwhelmed when confronted with more issues than they can feasibly handle. The Heart Talent loves to care about others. However, Heart Talents need to care for themselves first and not internalize every argument and interpersonal dynamic that exists in the company. Most Heart Talents find it hard to draw the line, set clear limits, and simply let go of people and situations beyond their control. They prefer to be of service when and where their talents are needed. Heart Talents may need to set boundaries and stop trying to be all things to all people. Saying "no" more frequently is often a positive step for the Heart Talent.

Wise Heart Talents have learned how to manage and protect themselves from those who will drag the organization down.

They know that if they dispense their caring energy in too many directions, they too will burn out. They avoid spending time worrying about situations beyond their control.

As a manager, you can help your Heart Talent employees set boundaries with peers and projects that consume them unnecessarily. Heart Talents benefit from the Club Talent's clear vision and clarity about structure, they are energized by the Diamond's creative mind, and they are grounded by the practical realism of a Spade Talent.

Heart Talent Work Preferences

Heart Talents like to work with others. Solitary work drains their energy. Ask Heart Talents to lead groups and oversee cross-functional projects. Ask them to advise you on people issues and solutions. The Heart Talent can be an excellent team spirit builder for a group in trouble. They are also exceptional coaches. Ideally, Heart Talents use their coaching and communication abilities to support the changes needed.

Regardless of their role in the organization, Heart Talents like to influence others and build collaborative relationships. They are especially good at motivating others and building an effective team. The Heart Talent is an ideal coach for those who want to develop skills in these areas. Heart Talents like to work on projects that have meaning and purpose. They get behind programs that make a difference in people's lives. Hearts are the natural Pied Pipers in the organization and others are willing to follow their lead.

The Heart-Type Organization

One Heart-type organization that is mission-driven is the Whole Foods Market. The vision of this company goes beyond the normal food retailer. Whole Foods Market is committed to creating a collaborative and interdependent community. They want their vendors, employees, and customers to be part of this community and encourage participants to communicate openly and with compassion. They celebrate the "breaking of bread" together and believe that eating healthy food is a source of joy in life. This amazing chain has astonished the marketplace with its exponential growth. Even the store itself is seen as a community gathering place where everyone is welcome. Whole Foods is an excellent example of a Heart-focused organization.

How to Lead Heart Talents

Heart Talents need a safe place to talk about the issues and concerns they observe. Without this outlet, they carry too much on their backs. They want your guidance about how much to get involved with issues and when to draw the line. Help Heart Talents set boundaries, limit priorities, and sort out how much they can expect from themselves. Watch for signs of burnout and invite Heart Talents to talk about their concerns to alleviate stress. Heart Talents benefit from receiving their own medicine. Hearts can offer you excellent advice about employee motivation and teamwork strategies. They have excellent insights about ways to approach different groups and individuals. Heart Talents want to know you appreciate their efforts to develop trust and build positive relationships within the organization.

Appreciate Each Employee's Unique Talent

Realize that most employees have a preferred talent. Identify which of the talent types best describes different employees. Encourage employees to take our online 360 Talent Assessment at *http://playtoyourstrengths.com/assessments/index.html* to discover their top talent strengths. Using this assessment, you can identify the composition of your team's talents and where you can leverage strengths and minimize potential weaknesses.

Your role as a leader is to help employees see the value of their talents and what they bring to the business. Encourage individuals to seek out opportunities to use their talents fully. Assign projects and work that utilize their talent strengths. Foster teamwork among the different talent types on projects and teams. Finally, share your best talent with employees and let them know how you can help them. Leaders and knowledge workers who leverage each other's talents are sure to succeed.

KEY HIGHLIGHTS FROM CHAPTER 5

- At different stages in a project, different talent types are needed.
- Diamond Talents like to think outside the box and create innovative solutions.
- Club Talents like to champion new ideas and set up structures to support the growth of a new vision.
- The Spade Talents like to "dig in" and get things done. They pay attention to implementation and the details.
- Heart Talents are good at motivating others, building teamwork, and gaining buy-in and commitment to projects.

Chapter 6

Deal with Talent Differences

TEAMS CAN RUN INTO TROUBLE when knowledge workers fail to deal with talent differences. Important projects can grind to a halt when individuals don't sync up their talents in productive ways.

The president of a small manufacturing firm called me to work with his leadership team. His staff wasn't working well together or meeting their business goals. A week before our first session took place, one of his team members, Ron, hit the wall. Ron had stood up in a meeting and yelled at the group, "I've had it. You will not give me one more thing to do!"

Later in the working session, we discovered the problem. Everyone on the team was a Diamond Talent except Ron. Ron was a Spade Talent. While his colleagues wanted to talk about long-term strategies and brainstorm solutions, Ron was the only get-it-done person on the team. By default, Ron was responsible for implementing everyone else's ideas.

This team's problems were corrected when the other leaders understood the talent type differences. They recognized they needed to limit their endless brainstorming and transition projects differently so Ron could execute their ideas. Ron was relieved—and more productive—when his team members stopped throwing their ideas over the wall and started working with him to ensure success. Recognizing the team's talent imbalance, and correcting it, made all the difference.

Set Others Up for Success

You can improve team performance by helping individuals recognize and leverage their talents. Simply being aware of talents is not enough. Individuals must accept responsibility for the end results—even when they play a minor part. Project success is achieved by smooth handoffs, coordination, and synergy. Like the game of volleyball, individuals set up the ball so that others can hit it over the net. The leader's role is to help employees orchestrate the right mix of talents to achieve the goals.

Strive for the Right Mix of Talents

In the quest to get things done, individuals and team members can overlook key talents necessary to achieve their goals. Chuck, the leader of a nonprofit organization, hired twenty people to work on a project. He later discovered that there was only one Heart Talent onboard. The newly formed team was predominantly Club and Spade Talents. Hence, the Club and Spade mindset dominated their meetings. There was little if any time spent talking about the need to gain stakeholder buy-in and commitment, or the necessity of building trust with suppliers. When the lone Heart individual on the team tried to raise these issues, his perspectives and point of view were ignored and undervalued.

To achieve a better team balance, Chuck decided to bring more Heart Talents onboard. At first, the Clubs and the Spades were agitated with the new discussions. They thought that dealing with the people issues would impede progress. But Chuck understood the power of having a more balanced team. He recognized that without a better balance, he would lose a vital key to commitment and results. Today, several years later, a Heart Talent leads this team and the group is performing admirably.

Recognize Too Much of a Good Thing

Maximizing employee talents is a balancing act. At any point you might have too much of one talent or not enough of another. For example, you may have too many Heart Talents on a team. When this happens meetings and discussions can become too emotional and process focused. Every topic is subject to endless rounds of circular discussions. Lots of energy is devoted to how everyone is feeling. However, not enough energy is directed toward the task at hand and on moving the agenda forward.

Conversely, a team comprised primarily of Spade Talents concentrates exclusively on the work itself. They don't have time for meetings. They don't see why they should meet at all. After all, meetings just take time away from the real work. When Spades do come together, they often run through a series of checklists, asking, "Is this done? Is that done?" Spade discussions are about tactics. Dialogue about the vision, employee morale, and personnel policies are frequently not on the agenda. It's the work itself that motivates and propels Spades. But Spade types can miss important issues of sustenance.

Hold a meeting dominated by Club Talents and you'll see a lot of wheeler-dealers who design plans for the future. However, an overabundance of Clubs can mean that immediate issues are not being addressed. For Club Talent individuals, the here and now concerns are not fun and take away precious time from bigger plans.

Diamond Talents add innovation. But too many Diamonds on a team can create more ideas than can possibly be implemented. Diamonds can also disrupt projects that are already under way by throwing in their latest bright idea. Diamonds need to be aware when suggesting one more idea is not helpful and interferes with progress.

Notice When Talents Are Either Under- or Overplayed

There's a right time and place for each talent contribution—the right balance is essential for success. The chart on the following page outlines the contribution of each talent and identifies what happens when there is either too much or too little of a talent type. To be most effective, leaders need to strive for the right balance and mix of the four talent types.

Each talent type needs to associate with other talent types to gain their perspective and achieve project goals. Though it is more comfortable for employees to stay with their own talent types, they need to interact. When Diamond Talents collaborate with Spade Talents, they can observe firsthand how their innovative ideas translate into challenging projects. The Diamond Talent might realize he's added too many bells and whistles. So the next time around, he can avoid burdening others with intriguing but otherwise impractical ideas. As different talent types work together, they become attuned to one another's needs and boundaries.

It's especially important for employees to associate with others who are strong in their weakest talent. Typically, employees are weak in one or two of the four talent areas. When individuals connect with others who have skills that they don't, it increases their perspective and sensitivity to what's needed for project success.

MAXIMIZE EMPLOYEE TALENTS

DIAMOND TALENT	TOO LITTLE	TOO MUCH
Imagine new possibilities	Stuck with the status quo	Too many ideas
Think outside the box	Lack of innovation	Brainstorming but no actions
Challenge the status quo	Outdated product and services	Ideas are not practical
Discover innovative solutions	Risk averse	Disrupt orderly process
Creative problem solving	Missed opportunities	No process
Innovation		Confusion and scrambling

HEART TALENT	TOO LITTLE	TOO MUCH
Build trust	Lack of teamwork	Ignore data and facts
Develop others	Mistrust and silos	Often burned out and overwhelmed
Express appreciation	Low enthusiasm	Sluggish decision-making
Resolve conflicts	Conflicts and in-fighting	Strive to please everyone
Secure commitment	Low morale	No tough decisions made

CLUB TALENT	TOO LITTLE	TOO MUCH
Lead change	New ideas fizzle	Unnecessary change
Champion ideas	Missing leadership	Blind ambition
Design strategies	Lack of vision	Lack of concern for people
Set up structure	Inadequate resources	No buy-in to changes
Secure resources	Few systems in place	Power politics

SPADE TALENT	TOO LITTLE	TOO MUCH
Complete projects	Incomplete projects	Missing larger strategy
Manage cost and schedules	Projects are chaotic	Ignore people needs
Improve processes	Constant firefighting	Not creative
Document plans	Details missing	All task focused
Solve immediate problems	Duplication of effort	Missed opportunities

Eliminate the "It's Not My Job!" Mindset

When employees spend time doing the work of other talent types, they feel like they're not doing "real" work. To a Spade, the Diamond's work of designing plans five years into the future is not real work. The Spade is dealing with projects that are due next week—not next year. To a Diamond, thinking about the mundane details of daily logistics is not "real work"—whereas landing a big account or developing a new product is.

A Spade Talent who is doing Heart Talent work—such as team building—will feel as if it's all a big waste of time. They think, "When is this going to be over so I can get back to my real job?" The truth is that all talent types are necessary and each does real work. All talent types are necessary for a strong team. Employees need to appreciate the perspectives and priorities of other talent types.

Ensure Accountability

Everyone must be responsible for the end goal. Just because individuals do their part, it doesn't mean they're off the hook. You must help knowledge workers recognize that once they do their part, they're not done. A Diamond might think, "I've just made an incredible breakthrough! Why do I need to get bogged down with the mundane details?" However, the Diamond Talent still needs to ensure a smooth handoff to someone else, usually a Club or a Spade, who will take the ball and run with his or her idea. As the leader, you must recognize the ego challenges that crop up as individuals with different talent types work together. There's a strong tendency for each talent type to see her or his contribution as the most important. You can address this dynamic by visibly acknowledging what each talent type contributes to the project. Reinforce that everyone is responsible for achieving the end goal.

Stay Involved in Project Handoffs

As a leader, you may need to get directly involved in handoffs from one group to another. Transitions from marketing to sales, or from design to engineering, or editing to production are often fraught with problems. Don't assume the goals are met when your employees complete their part of the assignment. Make sure they know what happens when the project moves into another area. Hold employees accountable for the success of the whole project—not just their individual piece of it. It's easy for blame to arise when groups are passing work back and forth. Help employees recognize the challenge of handoffs, respect talent differences, and take responsibility for overall results

Value the Kaleidoscope of Talents on Your Team

It's the lively exchange and combination of talents that brings the greatest value—not any one talent alone.

♣ **Without Clubs,** new initiatives never get off the ground.

♠ **Without Spades,** projects run over time and budget.

♥ **Without Hearts,** there's high turnover and low morale.

♦ **Without Diamonds,** there's no innovation or new ideas.

When any one of the talents is missing, there are unmet business needs.

Success happens when Diamond researchers work with Spade implementors to complete a project; or when the Club Talent champions the Diamond's innovative idea and makes it real; or when the Heart Talent builds trust and teamwork that enables the Club Talent to achieve his or her vision. It's the interchange, and leveraging, of talents that produces the greatest results.

LEVERAGING TALENTS IMPROVES SALES RESULTS

Recently a group of sales professional attended one of my training seminars. In this session, participants took the Play to Your Strengths Talent Assessment and discovered that 75 percent of them were predominately Heart and Spade Talents. But they were losing business to their competitors. As Heart/Spade salespeople, they were great at keeping in touch, following up, and building relationships with their customers.

However, to be effective in today's market, they needed to develop more Club and Diamond abilities. Their customers wanted innovative ideas to help them take their business to the next level. Customers wanted Clublike strategies that would help their company become more profitable. With this knowledge of talents, the salespeople saw what they were missing. They decided to add more Club and Diamond abilities to their repertoire—while leveraging their natural talents as Hearts and Spades. By aligning their talents with customer needs, they were able to take their business to the next level.

Mesh Talents and Organizational Culture

It's important to recognize that your culture may not welcome all talent types. Some organizations don't want a lot of teamwork. And some companies prefer to stick with the tried and true. The classic example is Henry Ford at Ford Motor Company. He declared that customers could have any color they wanted, "as long as it was black." General Motors used to stamp out the same kinds of cars even though consumers wanted a wide variety. But later, the company proved to be more responsive and captured a huge section of the market.

If your organization is not supportive of an individual's talent, encourage the employee to adapt to but not adopt the culture around them. I've seen very talented individuals shrink because they're in a culture that does not welcome their talents. A Diamond Talent tucked inside a get-it-done Spade culture will struggle to feel appreciated. Stay in communication with these employees and help them weigh the impact of being in a culture that does not welcome their talents. At some point the cost of staying may be too high. When this is the case, encourage employees to look for another position more suited to their talents.

Diamonds Want to Be Creative

Diamond Talent individuals want to create innovation. In some organizations that may be welcomed—or it may not. At Apple Computer, founder Steve Jobs's flurry of ideas was too discomforting for the establishment-minded leadership. The company offered him a VP position at Apple. But Jobs wasn't interested in playing small. He turned down the job and launched a new company called NeXT Computer—which Apple later bought from him for $400 million. Diamond Talents thrive in organizations that support innovation and risk taking.

Club Talents Want to Climb Mountains

Club Talents are natural change agents. Clubs often meet resistance simply because they are making waves. But making waves is the Club Talent's stock and trade. A Club leader will have few qualms about outsourcing a whole division if that's what's needed. The Club knows that implementing a new system often means clearing out the old. Successful Clubs learn how to engage others and minimize resistance to change. They use their Club power to reach out and engage the right people. Club Talents thrive in organizations that want growth and change.

Heart Talents Want a Positive Work Climate

Heart Talent individuals can get short shrift in a rapid-fire, "make it happen" organization that's focused strictly on the bottom line. In this environment, Hearts find it hard to contribute in a meaningful way. There is scant recognition for the time and effort they spend motivating, developing, and inspiring their staff.

In an insurance organization, a Spade CEO was so task-oriented and bottom-line driven that her staff and employees rebelled. They threatened to go to the board and complain about this leader's harsh manner with employees. The CEO did not want trouble with the board. But neither did she want to change her style.

To address this situation, I advised this CEO to turn over the leadership of the company to her staff. Eventually she hired three Heart Talent leaders who had exceptional people skills. Thus, the CEO was able to stay focused on her strengths and rely on others to lead employees. In organizations firmly focused on the bottom line, Heart Talents play a vital role. Hearts thrive in organizations that want employees to feel inspired, work as a team, and bring their best to the business.

Spade Talents Want Orderly, Efficient Processes

Spade Talents may have less trouble fitting in and being accepted in a culture, because their work is tied to immediate goals. The Spade's work usually runs with the grain of the organization. Spades are busy getting things done. The challenge for

Spade Talents is when they work in a culture that believes in working crisis to crisis. Spades may feel undermined when they try to bring order to the mess. Spade Talents need to feel respected, and they need to have their ideas and suggestions heard. They want to receive the support necessary to solve the problems.

A Spade Talent can also be overlooked. Their long hours and hard work can easily be taken for granted. Others assume that the Spade will dig in and get things done. Once in a while Spades need to look up and see where they are going—and even call attention to the good work they are doing. Be sure to recognize their contributions and hard work. The Spade Talent thrives in a culture where their ideas are heard and actions are taken to remove barriers to performance.

Help Employees Sell Their Value

As the leader, you can help employees see the value of their talent's unique contribution to the business. Sometimes individuals may not feel appreciated. Often these people don't know how to communicate what they and their talents bring to the table. They then wonder why others don't appreciate what they offer. For example, a Spade who points out every flaw in the team's plan believes she is providing useful information. This information, given at the right time and place, is invaluable and could help the team avoid mistakes. However, if the Spade does not consider her audience, the timing, and the value of what she is saying, others will not appreciate her contribution.

When employees share their talent, they need to think of the receiver. You can help the Spade prepare others for what she is about to say and wait for the appropriate time to share her observations. You must help employees recognize when they are flinging their talents at others. Encourage knowledge workers to first stop and consider what the other person or department needs and wants. Help employees recognize whether their talent is right for the situation. Finally, coach employees to communicate the value of their talents to others and how it benefits their organization, department, or project. Many knowledge workers need to learn how to correctly position their talents so they are received and appreciated.

As the leader you can help them identify the right fit for their talents by asking, "What problems do you love to solve? What challenges do you like to address? What projects have your name on them?"

- When everyone is conducting "business as usual," ask the Diamonds how they can add value. The Diamond Talent might say to others, "I can see new possibilities. If you're in a rut, bring me in. I can offer you new solutions and ideas that will help your project succeed."

- The Spade Talent says, "Call me when you have lots of good ideas but need to focus on one of them and bring it across the finish line."

- The Heart Talent says, "If people are tiptoeing down the halls instead of working together, I can turn this situation around."

- The Club Talent might say, "Call me when you have a big idea. I can help you transform your vision into reality."

Each person must clarify and communicate the merits of her or his talent contribution to others. Employees must let others know how and when they can add value to situations. Your job is to help knowledge workers recognize the value of their talents and find ways to communicate their offering to others.

Doing so means recognizing the four talent types and where each one contributes value to your organization. Appreciating talent differences empowers every member of the team to bring his or her best to the business.

KEY HIGHLIGHTS FROM CHAPTER 6

- Employees must do more than their part. They must accept responsibility for the end result.
- Make sure team projects have the right mix of talents to meet business needs.
- Recognize and remedy tensions caused by talent differences—especially during project handoffs.
- Encourage employees to communicate the value of their talents to others.
- Help employees leverage each other's talents to achieve the best outcomes.

Chapter 7

Leverage Personal Attributes

YOU MAY RECALL the television commercial of a few years ago for Nikon cameras. In it, tennis star Andre Agassi scurries around a tennis court while being photographed. He then points the camera at the audience and says, "Image is *everything.*" In business and in life, others immediately pick up on the image that we project.

Our image is conveyed by our personal attributes. Attributes describe our way of being, and how we come across to others. Personal attributes can strengthen or weaken a knowledge worker's contribution. Attributes should not to be confused with talents. Talents are the various activities and task preferences that an individual does to get work done. Attributes describe how the person relates to others. Some individuals are "steady and reliable," while others are "inspiring and creative." Attributes are what others experience when they connect with us. For knowledge workers, personal attributes create a perception that they are either "easy and manageable" or "challenging and difficult" to work with.

Attributes Enhance Talents

Attributes affect our contribution. Two individuals are successful project managers—one is viewed as "courageous," while the other is seen as "logical." Both individuals are strong performers. But the contribution of the *logical* project manager is going to be different from that of the *courageous* project manager. Another employee's talent might be teaching, while her main attribute is compassion. Clearly a *compassionate* trainer will have a different impact on participants than a *pragmatic* trainer.

Ask employees to name their primary talent, such as being an *innovator*, and then name their top attribute, such as *patience*. Put the talent and attribute together, and the employee describes himself as a "patient innovator." Someone else on the team might be an *insightful listener*, a *critical thinker*, a *steady mediator*, an *over-the-top presenter*, a *powerful designer*, a *logical planner*, or a *calm organizer*. Once employees have the two talent and attribute words that best fit them, they can then translate this into what they offer to others. Ask the employee, "What value do you bring to others because you are a patient innovator?" Suppose an employee is a *creative problem solver*. This person can help the team quickly think of new ideas to ensure progress.

Attributes Can Be an Asset or a Liability

An employee's ability to contribute to the organization is very much shaped by her attributes. Moreover, knowledge workers, while having an abundance of talent, often have attributes that can make them hard to manage or rub teammates the wrong way. Employees must learn to recognize personal attributes and actively manage them so they become an asset—not a liability.

I learned about attributes early in my career. At the time I was working for a large corporation. I wanted to leave my human resources position and take a position in marketing. But before offering the position to me, the senior vice president wanted to learn about my capabilities and reputation. So he asked one of his staff members to interview five to seven people who had worked with me over the years. The interviews took place and I was invited to lunch to hear the results. I was shocked to hear what he told me. He said, "Faith, people either love you or hate you. Most people think that you walk on water and that you're tremendously capable. However, there were a few people we interviewed that said they disliked your independent style and constant lobbying for change. No one who knew you had a non-chalant attitude. It was either love or hate."

At the time, I had no idea others were upset with me or that I was perceived as a threat. The interviewer then told me, "Based on this information, we've concluded that you *are* a change agent. So, we want to offer you the job."

Although I got the coveted position, I realized that my attribute of being a maverick was also a weakness and causing unnecessary angst for colleagues. My "get it done at all costs" approach was creating problems.

I was lucky. I received useful informative about the flip side of my maverick attribute early in my career—before it created irreparable damage. However, the subject of attributes is usually off-limits and not something that is discussed openly in corporate life. And if we do talk about someone's attributes, it's usually behind his or her back. The impact of employee attributes cannot be underestimated. How well knowledge workers manage personal attributes often has more bearing on their success than education, talent, or technical expertise.

Create Your Personal Brand

Attributes can differentiate you from your colleagues and peers—though not always in a positive way. When one of your employees walks into a room, how are they perceived? Is the individual perceived as easy to get along with or as a trouble-maker? The following story illustrates how even positive attributes can cause trouble if not managed effectively.

A project manager named Marta worked for a chemical company in Pennsylvania. She had fifteen people reporting directly to her. Others described Marta as "calm," "pleasant," and "low-key." Marta recruited talented people for her team. She hired well and trained her employees to take charge. She continually coached and offered her staff ongoing support to help them succeed in their jobs. As a result, her department ran smoothly.

Largely through her efforts, Marta's group implemented their projects successfully. Yet, when it came time to promote someone to the manager position, Marta was overlooked.

Because Marta was calm and low-key, others assumed she wasn't doing that much! They assumed she just lucked out and got all the good people in her department. Her employees were also taken for granted and expected to excel.

Being passed over was a huge wake-up call for Marta.

She took time to reflect on what was happening to her career and learned about talents and attributes. Though incredibly capable, Marta realized her efforts were invisible. No one saw or appreciated all the work she had put into developing her staff. Her naturally calm nature was becoming a disadvantage.

Marta did not want to change her natural style—nor should she. But she did need to manage the impact of her easygoing attributes. So she went to see her boss and said, "Because I'm naturally low-key, it's easy to overlook my part in the success of this department. I want you to know that I swim like a duck; on the surface my movement looks effortless, but below water I'm paddling like crazy. I've turned five projects around in three years. We've gone from a 45 percent response rate to 95 percent.

In other words, the success we're having is a direct result of the people I've hired and the development they've received. I'm confident I can work wonders like this anywhere I go. I don't want to be underestimated or overlooked because of my calm, relaxed style."

For the first time, her boss took notice. Within three months, Marta received a big promotion. But first she had to take charge and let others know that her natural style was what made all the difference in her department. She had to take charge and communicate her value to others. Her attributes, or "way of being," turned out to be the secret ingredient that enabled her team and projects to succeed.

Attributes can be tremendous *enhancers* of employee talents, but they can also be *inhibitors*.

Manage Attributes As Well As Talents

Attributes impact performance and affect teamwork. Managing attributes is more important with knowledge workers, because you know they're smart, talented, and educated—that's a given. But they are also highly ego-driven and independent. Thus, attributes become the make-or-break factor for career success.

As a leader of knowledge workers, you need to bring the subject of attributes into the open. All too often, conversations about an employee's attributes are done at the water cooler or after the employee has a serious problem. As the leader, you can help employees recognize how important attributes are to their success. Here are some ways to bring this topic to the forefront:

- **Coach employees to manage attributes.** Notice employees' positive attributes and also help them recognize the flip side—or weakness—in this attribute.

- Include attributes in performance review conversations and talk explicitly about behaviors that are helpful and those that are not. How employees manage their attributes should be just as much a performance issue as talent and skill.
- Help team members recognize positive attributes in each other and the value that each person brings to the team.
- Invite team members to be direct with each other and talk candidly about each other's positive and negative attributes.
- Encourage employees to ask others how they are perceived and seek recommendations about how to improve their effectiveness.

Easy Ways to Discover Your Attributes

One way to discover attributes is surprisingly simple. Get a hold of a list of adjectives—like the one that follows—and simply circle the attributes that you feel best describe you. Taking your time and being as thoughtful as possible, rate yourself. What attributes best describe you? Try to limit yourself to five attributes so you don't have an endless list.

You can also ask friends and peers to undertake the same exercise for you. Ask them to identify your best attributes. If a consensus arises about what your top three to five attributes are, stop right there. Follow up and ask questions to learn more about how you are perceived. Be curious and you'll gain valuable information. Once you have completed this exercise, ask employees to do the same exercise for themselves. You may also want to ask employees to select what they consider to be their key attributes and compare it against what attributes their peers selected for them. This is a valuable way to discern if perceptions mesh.

One of my clients took the time to ask her closest colleagues and friends to describe her best attributes. To her utter amazement she discovered that what her peers appreciated most was her calm nature. For much of her life she thought of herself as dull and boring. But her friends reframed this erroneous notion and helped her see the value of her calm nature.

LIST OF ATTRIBUTES

Assertive	Diplomatic	Logical
Precise	Daring	Cooperative
Courageous	Risk taker	Intuitive
Gregarious	Persuasive	Organized
Wise	Persistent	Easygoing
Compassionate	Determined	Authentic
Spontaneous	Systematic	Confident

You can use the Play to Your Strengths Attribute and Talent system to help your team explore their attribute and talent strengths. Visit my Web site at *www.playtoyourstrengths.com* to learn more about this easy and fun way to discover attribute and talent strengths.

Solicit Peer Feedback on Attribute Strengths

Another technique for determining employee attributes in a team setting is to have each person take turns telling a one-minute story to the group. The subject matter of the story isn't important. It's how the employee tells the story that matters. After each story, ask team members to write down the attributes of the storyteller, as they perceive them. Ask participants to share only positive attributes with the speaker.

The beauty of this method is that it doesn't matter whether or not the people in the group know each other. Even when people aren't acquainted with one another, it's amazing how many participants pick similar attributes to describe the storyteller. When conducting this exercise, invite participants to write down two types of attributes. Identify the person's "visible" and "invisible" attributes. Invisible attributes are traits that may not be easily noticed or definable.

It behooves you as a leader to know what your chief attributes are. Knowing your attributes helps you recognize the helpful qualities you bring to your team and colleagues, and as a result you'll appreciate your unique way of leading others.

Develop a Powerful Contribution Statement

Once employees have defined both their talents and attributes, ask them to create a Contribution Statement. A Contribution Statement is a headline or sound bite that tells others what they have to offer. Even if employees never say it out loud, it's still helpful for them to do this exercise because it helps them clarify in their own minds the value they offer to your organization.

If employees don't see how their talents and attributes add value, invite team members to speak up and tell them. Encourage team members to share their Contribution Statements and refine them. Instruct employees to be specific about their unique contributions. Some will consider this exercise bragging, but in reality it helps others to know where they can contribute.

It's not enough for an employee to know she has talent as an "inventor" or "designer." Employees must be able to translate their talents into a "what's in it for you" statement that means something to others in the organization. Customers and departments don't want to know what an individual's talents are—they want to know how they will *benefit* from the individual's talents. To create a Contribution Statement that conveys their value, employees must look to the customer. Creating a great Contribution Statement requires knowledge workers to solicit feedback about the value they bring to a department or process and incorporate that into their Contribution Statement.

To create a Contribution Statement, use the following template as a guide. First pick your favorite attribute from the list of five you selected earlier. Then pick your top talent. Choose one attribute and one talent only.

YOUR CONTRIBUTION STATEMENT TEMPLATE

- I AM A:

  _____

  Insert favorite attributes. Identify your unique characteristics: innovative, creative, clear-headed, easygoing, determined, sensible, accurate, inspiring, etc.

- WHO LIKES TO:

  _____

  Name the talents you constantly use: analyzer, problem solver, coach, planner, organizer, inventor, motivator, etc.

- DESCRIBE THE CONTRIBUTION YOU MAKE TO OTHERS:

  _____

  Insert what you do. I help you resolve problems, discover new ideas, move off the dime, launch projects, and integrate ideas.

- CALL ME WHEN:

  _____

  Describe the symptoms or problems that indicate your talents are needed.

- I CAN HELP YOU:

  _____

  Tell them how you can help them.

Remember to keep your initial Contribution Statements simple and compelling. Here are a few examples:

SAMPLE CONTRIBUTION STATEMENTS

- I am a *creative problem solver* who helps others implement their ideas. Call me when you have sticky problems you want resolved. I can help you figure out what to do.

- I am a pioneering researcher who helps others appreciate new solutions. Call me when you need stakeholder buy-in on a new technology. I make it easy for others to accept new ideas.
- I am an inspirational coach who helps others launch new endeavors. Call me when you are having trouble getting people to embrace change. I love to motivate employees to try a different way of doing things.

Speak Up about Your Value

Ask team members to share their Contribution Statements. Encourage employees to describe how their talents help peers, customers, and other groups.

The key to creating a great Contribution Statement is for employees to recognize how their talents help others succeed. If the knowledge worker is a critical thinker, she might say, "I can help you anticipate problems so you don't get blind-sided." If another is a great organizer, this person might say, "I can help you organize this so you can spend time on the real priorities." If still another is an insightful coach, she might say, "I help leaders speed up implementation." To create a great Contribution Statement, employees must think from the other people's point of view and highlight the benefits from their vantage point.

Ensure Employee Talents Are Visible

Too many knowledge workers feel underused, undervalued, and unappreciated. And indeed others are not using their services to the best advantage. As a leader, you can help employees sharpen their message and clearly communicate to others the value they bring. When employees are not selected for premier projects that are right up their alley, nine times out of ten, they haven't expressed interest or clarified what they offer. Knowledge workers must let others know where they can add value. Once this happens, others will seek them out for their unique abilities. Advise employees to slip their Contribution Statement into conversations. Soon it becomes part of the informal chitchat with others. This simple message communicates what they offer. Ideally, it's succinct. It stands out. And others remember it.

Knowledge workers want to do meaningful work. You can help them shine the light on their talents, manage their attributes, and articulate the value they bring. Ultimately it's up to the knowledge worker to use their abilities wisely. And when they do, they'll get the cooperation they need to implement their projects. Successful knowledge workers know their talents, their impact on others, and what they contribute to the business.

KEY HIGHLIGHTS FROM CHAPTER 7

- Attributes are our "style," or way of being. Personal attributes can help or hinder our performance.

- Employees need to solicit feedback and learn how others perceive them.

- It's the employee's job to communicate the value they bring.

- A Contribution Statement lets others know what you offer and how they will benefit from your services.

- Once employees are clear about their contribution, others will catch on quickly.

Chapter 8

Discover Your Success Pattern

HAS AN EMPLOYEE ever said to you, "Let me do it my way!" As mentioned earlier, knowledge workers, in particular, don't like to be told how to do their job. If you try to force them into a mold or insist they do it a prescribed way, you're likely to encounter rebellion, poor morale, and high turnover.

A colleague of mine, Jill, was a sales rep in a large corporation. Her boss routinely looked over her shoulder asking if she had made the "required number" of sales calls that day. She gave lip service to her boss about doing what was asked of her, but in reality Jill made very few outbound calls. She had discovered a method that was more effective for her in generating sales. Instead of making thirty phone calls a day, she researched customers and discovered what their needs were. Then she targeted a few customers with persistence until she made the sale. Though she was the highest sales producer in the region, her boss did not approve of her methods because his belief was more calls equal more sales. He rated her poorly in her performance review, saying she lacked "closing skills." But Jill had discovered her own way which worked extremely well. Despite her poor performance rating, Jill was nominated for International Rookie of the Year in honor of her astonishing sales success. Today Jill is a well-known sales consultant who helps others learn her winning formula. Her independent thinking is still paying off for her.

Everyone Has a Success Formula

Knowledge workers have a personal formula for success, or what I call a success pattern. A success pattern is the way you sequence your top talents to achieve your goal. Jill's success pattern was to research leads, learn about her customer, hone in, and persistently pursue the client until she closed the sale. Her boss's success pattern was call, call, and call. His experience was that the more clients you reached, the more you sold. And actually both ways *can* work. They are just very different success patterns.

How Talents Fit into the Success Formula

Learning about the four talent types gave you a broad understanding of the four talents needed to get projects done. But to understand your employees' success patterns, you must break down these four talents into more specific subtalent abilities:

CLUB TALENT includes the subtalents of envisioning change, forming partnerships, and securing funding.

HEART TALENT includes the subtalents of appreciating others, promoting teamwork, and coaching others.

SPADE TALENT includes the subtalents of organizing projects, monitoring progress, and handling the details.

DIAMOND TALENT includes the subtalents of researching, brainstorming, and designing.

An individual's success pattern describes the sequence in which they use their top four to six talents to achieve a goal. Everyone has a slightly different success pattern that influences how quickly they make decisions, and whether they want to work alone or involve others. Success patterns develop as a result of our experiences and learning what works for us.

Lay Out Your Success Pattern

Most employees have one primary talent and roughly four to six supporting talents. You can discover a knowledge worker's primary talent by asking her or him, "Which talent do you enjoy using first and foremost?" For example, knowledge workers who primarily use their Heart Talent of coaching may also have good planning, influencing, and detail management skills—but they use these other talents to support their coaching work. Ask employees, "What are your top four to six talents that you use most often?" "How do these talents support your primary talent?"

Evan's Success Pattern

Here's an example of one employee's success pattern. Evan is a Club Talent and her supporting talents are researching, influencing, and facilitating.

- Champion (Club is her primary talent)
- Research (Diamond)
- Influencer (Heart)
- Facilitator (Heart)

Evan loves to champion new initiatives. However, she is also strong in three other supporting talents. She uses these additional talents to support her primary work of championing new initiatives.

The first thing Evan does when she champions a new initiative is to conduct extensive research on the new idea utilizing her Diamond Talent abilities. Once she is convinced that the idea is a good one, she advocates for it with her Club talents. As the project champion, she uses her Heart talents to gain commitment and buy-in. Throughout the project, Evan's Heart and Club Talents work hand in hand to ensure success. Once the idea is approved, Evan likes to stay involved and use her Heart facilitator talent to ensure successful implementation. This success pattern enables Evan to achieve her best results. Her greatest ability is championing new initiatives and seeing them succeed. She uses her supportive talents to ensure this happens.

On projects she is asked to champion, she always wants to do research first. The research step is critical for her to be successful. Without this step in her success pattern, she would not be convinced the idea was a good one. And she would not be able to champion it. Another knowledge worker could have an entirely different success pattern. This person might be able to jump in without any research and champion a new idea successfully. A gut feeling is all this person needs to lead the charge. But for Evan, the research activity is critical to her success.

Each person draws upon his or her individual success pattern to achieve their goals. Individuals will proceed in different and unique ways—even if they are pursuing an identical goal. Knowing your employee's or coworker's individual success pattern is helpful when you are collaborating on projects together. It will help you achieve the desired goal in the best possible way—without unnecessary conflict.

Success Patterns Operate Behind the Scenes

We can't see someone's success pattern from the outside. Others less involved with Evan might say she jumped into championing the new project too quickly, or that she needlessly got people excited about some half-formulated, risky proposal. However, they may not realize how thoroughly she researched the idea.

Coworkers may only encounter Evan for the first time when she's in the Heart facilitator mode. Thus, they might not realize how much Diamond Research time and effort she's invested in the project. They only see her as the day-to-day project facilitator. Knowing each other's success pattern helps employees work more collaboratively and effectively as a team. Teammates will respect each other's way of getting things done and know how to accommodate and support each other's unique success pattern.

The Sequence of Your Talents Is Crucial

To identify your success pattern as the leader, look at the following list of talents. These are some of the talents that leaders and employees draw upon to implement new projects. While not exhaustive, the twenty-five talents listed are enough to get you started. From this list, pick five to seven of your top talents.

- Synthesizer
- Researcher
- Coordinator
- Motivator
- Developer
- Analyzer
- Humorist
- Advocate
- Truth-teller
- Monitor
- Inspector
- Planner
- Implementer

- Storyteller
- Facilitator
- Designer
- Coach
- Teacher
- Translator
- Dealmaker
- Catalyst
- Visionary
- Champion
- Facilitator
- Mediator

Choose the talents you typically use when involved in a project. Next, write the name of each talent on a separate card. Finally, sequence the cards to show the order in which you are likely to use them. Ask yourself, "What talents do I use first, then second, or last, when I work toward a goal?" Feel free to add more talents to the previous list. Arrange your cards in a sequence that represents how you work. Be creative. Some individuals have a straight line of talents moving from left to right. Others have a pie-shaped sequence, and still others have talents they employ simultaneously. Make sure the sequence you arrange is meaningful to you. Ideally you will be able to take this pattern to your boss or colleagues and show them how you tackle major projects.

Key Questions to Ask

When doing this exercise, consider the following questions: How do you work through key decisions? Do you like to get involved first and then advocate for change? Do you plan upfront or think on your feet? We are all different in how we use our core talents! Find your preferred way of going about a project and getting it done. If you get stuck, think about a specific project that was successful and retrace the talents that you used to achieve your goal and the sequence in which you used them.

Perhaps you don't undertake the research step. You prefer to gather a lot of people and get ideas from them. You are at first a facilitator, then a champion, and finally a coach. So your pattern begins in a different way than the one previously discussed.

People Can Misunderstand Your Success Pattern

Suppose your success pattern for hiring a new employee involves many months of reflection and consideration about the right person to hire. You do extensive research on the ideal skills for the job. You write a detailed job description. Then you interview three individuals that seem to be the best candidates. But you make your final decision within the hour. In the months that follow, you are always pleased with your decision.

To employees who can't see your success pattern, it may look like you were impulsive. But were you? They may have no idea that you spent so much time researching the candidates and the needs of the position. Other employees are only aware of the interviews that took place and your quick decision. In reality, you were anything but impulsive. You were simply following the sequence of events that was most comfortable for you. Another manager might have asked for advice from a trusted colleague and gone with their choice—a different success pattern to be sure—but one that may work equally well depending on the situation.

Colleagues and peers who don't know the details of your unique process can misunderstand your success pattern—that's why it's important to communicate your success pattern to others.

Success Patterns Don't Change

Your success pattern is the natural, sequential order in which you use your top five to seven talents. This pattern remains constant despite the length of time a project takes. You will use the same pattern for important goals whether it takes a week or a year to achieve the desired outcome. Whether the project is urgent or indefinite in its duration, the success pattern that you follow remains intact. A manager in charge of a building reconstruction project will use the same success pattern to complete the project as he would to purchase a new car. Your basic behavioral patterns will reoccur. We all have a tried-and-true formula that works for us.

Study Your Past Successes

The next time you begin on a project, spend a few extra moments analyzing how you go about it. Diagnose the sequence of talents that you draw upon to move projects from start to finish. Notice the sequence in which you use your talents. The easiest way to understand your success pattern is to look at three big decisions you've made that have turned out well. Then, working from beginning to end, ask yourself, "What was the first thing I actually did to make this decision or project work well? What was the second thing? What was next?"

As you go through this mental review of steps taken—usually about five to seven steps in all—you'll see a pattern emerge. The sequence of talents you engage is similar.

Recognize Your Failure Pattern

Your failure pattern is visible when projects don't turn out the way you wanted or you are not able to realize your goal. Identifying your failure pattern is very instructive. It lets you know the steps essential to your success. To identify your failure pattern, consider decisions you've made that have turned out poorly or projects that have not gone well. Select three projects that did not work out to your satisfaction. Again, lay out the sequence of talents in your success pattern. Reflect on any missing steps. Notice how you may have followed your success pattern, but you gave short shift to one or two critical talents—or maybe you skipped over a talent entirely. Notice any common threads. Do you consistently skip over one step more than another? Identify the factors that set up this failure pattern.

For most employees, poor implementation and failure occurs when they have skipped one of the crucial steps in their success pattern. Sometimes others may persuade the employee that a step wasn't really necessary. Or, the person simply didn't have time and skipped it. Then the project went south.

Because of time pressure the knowledge worker may have wanted to take a shortcut. Once you become aware of what is sabotaging your success pattern you can avoid it.

Keep in mind that success patterns can vary widely from person to person. Take the case of planning a project with a coworker. Your pattern and approach may be very different from that of your colleagues. The way your boss or employee goes about managing projects may drive you crazy. But before you dismiss their approach as faulty, ask yourself if they are truly proceeding in the wrong direction or if it is that you simply don't understand their success pattern?

DON'T FIGHT WITH SUCCESS.
A top executive asked me to conduct a team-building session for his executive staff. He was short on budget and wanted to cut corners. So he asked me to come into the session without interviewing key staff members. In my experience, unless I conduct up-front interviews with the participants, I don't believe I can be successful. Yet, I know other consultants who can just walk in and successfully lead a working session. Are they right and I'm wrong, or vice versa? No, It's simply that their success pattern is very different from mine.

My first response was, "I can't do this. The team is brand-new to me." Like everyone else, I was holding onto my success patterns. Based on my experience, I've learned that I need to interview the people ahead of time and understand their priorities in order to have a productive working session. This is what works for me.

I responded, "I'd still like to meet the team members and get to know their priorities. Then I'll develop an agenda and finalize the working session with you. When we've got this nailed down, I can lead the session." Despite pressure to cut corners, I stayed true to what I know works for me—and the sessions were a success.

Ask Employees to Share Their Success Patterns

Knowledge workers, in particular, do not like altering their success pattern. They may not have articulated it that way until now—but they do know they have a particular process or style of working. Learn how to work with them instead of against them by taking time to understand their success pattern. Also invite them to share with others how they like to work on a project. This basic understanding of success patterns and individual preferences will help team members work together smoothly.

Some employees need to think about decisions before taking action. They don't like to rush from one activity to the next. They need time for reflection and germination. One of their teammates, however, might be the type who's ready to jump right in. He or she enjoys being submerged in foreign territory. Which employee is right? Neither. They are both following their own dependable success pattern.

It also pays to notice how the success patterns of team members overlap or conflict. Ted, a project manager, flies through several of the early decisions rather easily. He is always waiting for the rest of the group. It's in everyone's best interest to know that. Perhaps Ted can be working on other assignments during the interim. That way, work is still getting done but other people have the time and space to reach their own conclusions.

One reason individuals seek out others is that they are actually seeking others who support their success pattern. When individuals with different success patterns work on the same project, it's important to find a reasonable balance. When success patterns collide, knowledge workers often don't recognize the invisible forces that are causing the problem. It's wise to advise employees to trust the success patterns of others, even though they are different from their own. Once employees understand one another's success patterns, they can learn to avoid a crash.

By helping employees understand one another's success patterns you can be sure they will have a better chance of working together. With an understanding of success patterns, knowledge workers can create greater team and project synergy.

The Leader's Success Pattern Dominates the Group

As a leader, it's important for you to realize that your success pattern is automatically the default success pattern for your group. This can pose a challenge for employees. You might be a leader who likes to take his time at the start of a project. But the rest of your group wants to go, go, go! However, it's your success pattern that prevails. The result is that team members will chew their nails and try to bottle their fast-start energy just to conform. On the other hand, a leader whose success pattern is more impulsive or "shoot-from-the-hip" might conflict with an employee who needs more data and research. Ideally you should work with your team to find a reasonable process that respects their needs.

A leader's success pattern has a major influence on how individuals and the team as a whole make decisions. A manager who needs lots of research upfront will also ask her people to gather research before making decisions. Likewise a facilitative manager who likes consensus will hesitate to make decisions without his whole team buying into the decision. And he'll expect his direct reports to do likewise. A leader's success pattern impacts the entire team. Be cognizant of this fact and recognize your impact on others. Take employee needs and success patterns into account when you are making big decisions.

Allow for Differences in Approach

As a leader, should you always seek out others with the same success pattern as yourself? After all, wouldn't that maximize your strengths and accelerate your progress? Maybe. But you're also increasing the risk that your weaknesses will derail the group. You incur unnecessary risks by working with similar success patterns. Sometimes more research and investigation are helpful. Other times, a decision needs to be made quickly. The talents, attributes, and success patterns others bring provide beneficial perspective and balance.

It's good for leaders to respect different success patterns of knowledge workers. A wise leader knows that regardless of who's on the team, the leader's success pattern tends to dominate. So, make sure you take time to recognize and respect the timing and work approach of others on the team. When you and employees know each other's success patterns, your group has the potential for far greater harmony and results.

Helping employees know their talents, attributes, and success patterns is like being able to drive at night with the headlights on. Knowledge workers can see the road ahead. They gain confidence in themselves and their approach. They know how to bring value to the organization. And they also recognize and appreciate one another's unique way of achieving results.

The results of understanding and managing for individual success patterns are:

- Increased job satisfaction
- Improved performance

- Faster, better results
- Higher retention
- Better use of resources

In this section you've learned how to discover your talents, recognize the four talent types, manage personal attributes, and work with success patterns. You now have a set of powerful tools for developing employees and leveraging their strengths. And you can fully appreciate the benefits of working together and collaborating to achieve project results. You've learned how to help employees communicate their value to others. And you have the tools to help them succeed.

The more knowledge workers shine, the easier and more productive your team will be. Now let's move on to the next section and you'll learn how to apply these ideas to leadership activities you're engaged in every day.

KEY HIGHLIGHTS FROM CHAPTER 8

- Every employee has a preferred way of working that works. This is called their talent success pattern.
- An individual's success pattern remains relatively constant. Typically, individuals use the same pattern when they make a key decision or a minor one.
- Understanding your success patterns helps you to be more productive and work collaboratively as a team.
- Don't take shortcuts with your success pattern. Failures happen when we neglect a certain talent that is key to our success.
- The leader's success pattern dictates the way that decisions are made by the group.

INNOVATORS　　　MOTIVATORS　　　ACTIVATORS　　　IMPLEMENTORS

Part 3

Play to Win

Chapter 9

Create a Winning Team

BUILDING A COHESIVE TEAM is hard in today's work environment. With increased workloads and commute times and decreased company loyalty and employee tenure, most employees consider "team spirit" a quaint notion from corporate days past. Getting knowledge workers to buy in to and invest the time in team building is particularly challenging. Why? Because knowledge workers see themselves as free agents. They don't expect to be with a company until retirement. Moreover, they can be highly competitive—and proprietary—about their ideas.

Ideally, you'd like more collaboration and participation from employees—as well as more enthusiasm, meaningful discussions, and tangible results. But employees often don't see the point of the investment. You want meetings to be productive and helpful. Yet, most of the time, half of the team members are missing because they have other demands on their time. And you end up doing most of the talking. Perhaps the only reason employees meet is because they all report to you. Otherwise they have nothing in common. Their projects are completely disparate and team members see little reason to be on the same team. Everyone feels relieved when the meeting is over because they can get back to their "real" work!

Find a Shared Purpose

How can you pull employees together in a meaningful way and have a dynamic team? And how can you leverage employees' collective talents to achieve your goals? You start by asking this question: "What can we do better together than we can alone?" If the answer is "nothing," then continue as you are. However, in order to be a dynamic, high-energy team, you need a shared purpose. Knowledge workers, in particular, need to feel that their daily work, tasks, and activities are connected to a bigger purpose and strategic objective for the organization.

Leaders often counter this by saying, "But my employees all work on different projects. We have no shared goals." You *must* have shared goals and a unifying purpose to leverage team members' talents. Without a shared purpose, you'll just be doing "team building"—and that won't last. A shared purpose—be it developing a new product, reducing costs by 25 percent, or being a top-five company in your industry—gives your team a solid reason to work together and leverage their abilities.

If you want to discover a shared purpose for your team, look at the needs of your customers and your business first. As mentioned earlier, your customers decide the value of what you offer. Start with customers as your focus—then move on to key strategies and leadership priorities.

Your team's shared purpose can relate to strategic priorities, organizational culture, leadership development, managing employees, or any topic relevant to business goals.

Following are examples of purpose statements related to different areas.

PURPOSE STATEMENTS RELATED TO CUSTOMERS

- We want to create a collaborative customer-focused culture.
- We want to be proactive with our customers instead of reactive.
- We want to say "yes" to customers and figure out win-win solutions.

PURPOSE STATEMENTS RELATED TO YOUR DIVISIONAL CULTURE

- We want to create an honest, caring environment for all employees.
- We want to become a seamless culture to serve our customers better.
- We want to help each other grow, develop, and succeed.

PURPOSE STATEMENTS RELATED TO STRATEGIC IMPERATIVES

- We want to cross-sell each other's products to our customers.
- We want to be a one-stop shop for doing business.
- We want to reduce our time to market with new products.

PURPOSE STATEMENTS RELATED TO LEADERSHIP DEVELOPMENT

- We want to develop extraordinary leaders who set the example for others.
- We want to retain and develop the high-talent leaders.
- We want to develop leaders who help the business grow.

PURPOSE STATEMENTS RELATED TO MANAGING EMPLOYEES

- We want to attract and retain the best and brightest employees.
- We want to improve performance and measure results.
- We want to better manage performance issues.

Key Questions to Discover Your Purpose As a Team

Pick one of these areas and then drill down with questions to find your shared purpose. Return to the question, "What can we do better together than we can alone—that absolutely needs to be done?" And remember, you only need one unifying purpose—not ten. Use the following questions to identify a purpose that's relevant for everyone on your team.

INTERNAL AND EXTERNAL CUSTOMERS

- What customers do we have in common?
- What issues or challenges do we face with our customers?
- What change do we all want to make in how we serve or relate to customers?

OVERRIDING STRATEGIC IMPERATIVES

- What aspect of the business strategy can we impact?
- What new direction or approach do we want to champion?
- What fundamental change is needed to achieve better bottom-line results?

DEPARTMENT AND TEAM CULTURE

- What do we want our workplace to be like?
- What values do we want to instill in others and ourselves?
- What behaviors and attitudes do we want to foster?

LEADERSHIP DEVELOPMENT

- What kind of leaders do we want to be?
- What knowledge and skills do we want to develop as leaders?

- What kind of example do we want to set for the next level of leaders?

MANAGING EMPLOYEES

- What challenges do we have in common related to managing employees?
- How do we lead employees in an empowering way?
- What mindset and behaviors do we all want to encourage in employees?

Look for pressing issues to identify a unifying purpose. The team's purpose should be germane to the needs of the business. Select a purpose that engages every member of your team.

Now with a team purpose in hand, you can go to work and build the kind of synergy and enthusiasm you only dreamed about.

Step 1: Meet Regularly

In order to create a high-performing team, team members must meet on a regular basis. One of the biggest deterrents to great team performance is that team members don't interact. Knowledge workers, in particular, are guilty of neglecting critical communication with their colleagues. Individuals are focused on their own goals. They don't take the time to look up and see the critical linkage of their project to other areas. When team members don't meet and connect on a regular basis, they end up duplicating efforts and missing opportunities. If staff meetings are optional, attendance drops off. It's essential that you have regular, mandatory meetings as a starting point. There's simply no way around this. If the meeting is good, the content is relevant, and employees attend, teamwork and results soar. But you must make team meetings a priority before this happens. Let your employees know that communication and collaboration with each other is important to their success.

Step 2: Identify Key Initiatives

With your shared purpose in hand, you're ready for the next step. It's time to select one to three initiatives you believe the team can accomplish. Let's say you decide that "creating a collaborative, customer-focused organization" is your shared purpose. Next, you want to hone in and pick a few initiatives that the team can actually achieve to make this concept real. In one organization, team members decided to talk directly to customers and discover what they liked and what they wanted to be different. In talking to customers, they learned that response time was not what it should be and that customers, and sales, were often lost to long waits. So they started to tighten up communication and collaboration among team members to improve response time. The key to picking initiatives is to find a few meaningful ones that will drive new behaviors and stretch team members to grow.

In another example, a management team's overriding purpose was to "ensure high performance and eliminate poor performance." For their initiative they decided to share challenges they were facing with employees and give each other ideas about how to address personnel issues. They also committed to learning and using a unified performance management approach throughout the division. Concrete projects are essential to make the larger team purpose come alive.

Step 3: Assess What a Project Needs

Look at the project and determine what talents are needed. What phase is the project in? Are you in start-up mode or is the project mature? Does the project need more creative ideas? Are you struggling to implement the project? Do you need to add structure to the idea? Or is it time to solicit buy-in from employees before going to the next phase?

Once you've assessed the project or initiative's needs, consider the talent types sitting around the table. Does the project require a Diamond mind to spark new ideas? Do you have individuals on the team who can spark new ideas? If not, what resources or staff can you bring in to stimulate the team's thinking?

If you don't have the talents around the table, you must provide this expertise to ensure the team's success. A roomful of Spade Talents is not going to generate a lot of innovative ideas without other sources. Are you in the implementation stage of the project? Great, then bring on the Spades and watch them go into action. Start using your knowledge about the four talent types to determine if you have the right competencies at the table for the task at hand.

A shared project makes it clear that different talents have more to contribute at different stages in the process. Allow this to be okay. Respect and value the individuals who launch the project and notice when their interest wanes. Make sure they are handing off to others who are eager to pick up the next phase and run with it. On shared projects, you want everyone to participate. But at different points, some will have more involvement than others.

Step 4: Leverage Team Member Talents

Now it's time to leverage team members' talents. Invite team members to step forward and share how their unique talents can help the team make progress on the key initiatives. Essentially, you're asking everyone to step up to the plate and claim the contribution they can make to achieve the initiatives and larger purpose. The key to success is challenging employees to select priorities that "have their name on it." You want their best talents at work here. So if you have a Heart Talent on the team, that individual might step forward and say, "I can help you gain buy-in to this idea." Or "I can develop a communication plan that ensures everyone understands why we are going in this direction." The Spade on the team might say, "I'd like to orchestrate a series of meetings with the customer so we can learn what they want from us." The Diamond might say, "I'd love to figure out an innovative way to respond to this challenge we're facing." Essentially you invite employees to step forward and contribute their best talents to key initiatives.

At this point you might want to revisit Chapter 7 and ask team members to develop a Contribution Statement. In a succinct way the Contribution Statement expresses the value that individuals bring to the team.

Encourage team members to pick a project that energizes them and feels important and meaningful to them. Ideally employee contributions are helpful in terms of visibility and experience. Their contribution must connect with what is meaningful to them as well as the business.

Step 5: Help Each Other Succeed

Ask individuals who have complementary talents to help each other. Some of the best leaders I know partner with others to complement their missing talents. Remember, 80 percent of individuals are low in at least one talent area. Partnering with others can help you cover the bases.

Realize, it's not always easy to partner with someone who is strong in your low-talent area. If you are a detail-oriented Spade, a creative Diamond who can't focus on one idea for more than five minutes could easily drive you to distraction. Learn how each of you approaches the task and what is the unique value you bring. Identify ways to work together and benefit from your different talents. Share your experience with the rest of the team. It takes work, communication, and appreciation of talent differences to collaborate—but the results are worth it.

If you are equally strong in all talent types, you may not be "exceptional" in any one. You're likely a generalist who sees what's needed and knows when a key talent is missing. Your best bet is to stay in the orchestrator role where you can oversee the project, assist in a variety of ways, and help others as an advisor or coach. If you're multitalented, avoid getting stuck performing any one talent for too long, as it will drain your energy. Be the generalist and help oversee and facilitate what's needed.

Ask for Group Feedback

Invite anyone who wants advice on a specific situation to take center stage. Give them five minutes to describe the challenge or opportunity. The rest of the team refrains from offering advice during this time. Team members may ask questions to clarify their understanding of the situation. However, guard against questions that are secretly offering advice, such as, "Do you think you should get more information?" This is an advice question that may easily have another agenda—not a question to clarify the situation.

Once the person has shared the challenging situation, he or she concludes by asking the group three to five key questions. Questions should always start with the words *what* or *how*? For example, *How can I achieve . . . ? What can I do about . . . ? What are your ideas and suggestions regarding . . . ? What can I learn from this . . . ? What is the best way to . . . ?*

Then the individual steps off center stage and sits quietly while each talent type on the team goes to work on his or her situation. It's important that the person asking the questions stays out of direct involvement in the discussion for the time being. Oftentimes, the focal person may initially resist solutions that other talent types come up with—particularly if they run counter to what the particular talent type finds comfortable. The purpose of the exercise is to let your team leverage their collective talents in solving the problem.

Once the team has deliberated, they present their ideas and suggestions to the focal person. During this presentation, the focal person listens and writes down all the ideas suggested. When the team is done, the focal person thanks the team for their insights, asks further questions, and comments on specific ideas she or he plans to implement.

The impact of this type of talent collaboration can be highly effective. In less than thirty minutes, the individual gains enough ideas, insights, and support to approach the problem or challenge constructively. And, perhaps more importantly, team members now have a stake in this person's success. This exercise is one of the best ways to leverage team members' collective talents and achieve meaningful results.

Maximize Talent Differences

Here are several ways to help employees benefit from the talent differences on your team: Ask employees to set development goals to leverage their talent strengths and manage talent weaknesses. Encourage individuals to use different talents than they normally do. If an individual is a Diamond who always comes up with new ideas, have her practice being a Spade and think about the details of implementation. Have the Diamond share what she learns from a Spade teammate. As the leader, you can ask, "What did you do that was different from your usual talent or success pattern? What were the results?"

Identify specific stakeholders and customers. See if you can figure out their talent type by reflecting on how they interact with you. Plan ways to connect with customers by relating to their talents. If you are talking to a Heart, take time to connect. If you are relating to a Spade, talk about projects and get into the details. If your customer is a Diamond, discuss new ideas. And if you are talking to a Club, talk about ideas that he is championing.

Take five minutes and ask everyone on the team to step into the role of a Spade, ask Spade questions, and give Spade responses. Do the same for each of the other types. Have the team members share what they learned and how it felt to be a different talent type.

Talk about tensions caused by missing talents and talent differences. Recognize the challenges of working with and accommodating differences. Ask what happens when Diamonds interrupt Spades? How can the Spades respond? What happens when Clubs make all the decisions? What can others do? What happens when Diamonds go off on a tangent? How do you intervene? What happens when there are no Hearts in the room? How do you compensate?

Plan ways to ensure a balance of talents on the team. Identify a time the team failed because they were missing one of the talent types.

Have each talent type join a group with others who have the same talent. Brainstorm the strengths and weaknesses of each talent type. Ask each group to share the strengths and weaknesses of their talent type with the larger group.

Enjoy Your High-Performing Team

Put these ideas into practice and your team will never be the same. As the team comes together, you'll have meetings that even you want to attend! Team members will feel less stressed and more connected to each other. The team's larger purpose will serve as a bridge that ties people, projects, and talents together. As a team, you'll learn how to collaborate and leverage your collective talents to achieve bigger goals.

KEY HIGHLIGHTS FROM CHAPTER 9

- Ideally, individuals on a team have a shared purpose. If your team doesn't have a shared purpose—create one.
- To be a high-performing team, your team must meet on a regular basis—no matter what.
- Make sure you have the right talents around the table to accomplish the tasks at hand.
- Focus on shared customers and outcomes to find a shared purpose.
- Encourage team members to recognize and appreciate talent differences.

Chapter 10

Develop Employees—
The Right Way!

LEGIONS OF KNOWLEDGE WORKERS are still trying to pursue a career ladder that no longer exists. They want to grow and develop, but the tried-and-true development strategies don't help them get far. The traditional management systems of performance appraisals, succession planning, and performance management continue to support outdated expectations and deficiency thinking. In a typical meeting related to an individual's career, the manager often asks:

- Where do you want to be in five or ten years?
- What are your career goals?
- What are your strengths and weaknesses?
- How will you remedy your weaknesses?

But these questions restrict the conversation rather than open it up. The employee feels they must say something "intelligent" about a three- to five-year plan, when perhaps they've given it little thought. Employees are asked to dwell on their weaknesses—which they hesitate to admit because it affects their salary. And studies confirm that investing in weaknesses yields a low return.

The Talent and Viability Approach

In today's environment, leaders can help employees more not by promising them a prescribed tenure with the company but by making sure they are viable in the marketplace. The biggest determinant of viability is talent. However, employees must also learn how to take charge of their careers and add value to the business. Thus, you need to ask your employees the following questions:

- What are your strengths?
- What challenges and opportunities interest you the most?
- Where and how can you contribute your best talents?

Here's the difference between a typical employee review meeting and a talent-focused discussion:

TWO DIFFERENT APPROACHES TO EMPLOYEE DEVELOPMENT

CAREER LADDER APPROACH	TALENT APPROACH
MANAGER: Where do you want to be in three to five years?	MANAGER: What are your best talents?
EMPLOYEE: How do you move up and get more money?	EMPLOYEE: Where can my talent produce the greatest results?
MANAGER: Address these deficiencies.	MANAGER: How will you leverage these strengths?
EMPLOYEE: What training do you want to take?	EMPLOYEE: Here are my ideas.
RESULTS: Low-impact bottom line	RESULTS: High-impact bottom line

If you're a manager from the old school, you might worry, "If we have a discussion with a talent focus, won't the knowledge worker wonder, 'Where is this heading?' Don't we need to look at the bigger, broader picture of the employee's career?"

There is definitely a time and place for career planning and reviews. Ideally, leaders have both career *and* talent-focused discussions. But the challenge with career planning is that the plan can become obsolete before the employee walks out of the office. Three to five years from now, and certainly ten years down the road, is far into the future considering the way business and society are changing.

Ensure Viability in the Marketplace

Your first job as a manager is to help employees recognize their talents. Talent has more equity than stock options or pensions in today's marketplace. Once employees know their talents, have them ask themselves, "Where can my unique abilities make a difference to the business?" Advise them not to wait for the perfect job to use their talents. Ideally, employees should look for ways to contribute their talents everywhere they go. Let talent determine the parameters of their job and career trajectory. The best career opportunities are more likely to come when employees are doing what they love than from internal job postings.

Find Out Where You Add Value

Many knowledge workers don't know their value because they have never taken the time to recognize their impact. Seeing the impact of our talents means knowing, in no uncertain terms, how our talents contribute to results. Specifically, if the person is a Heart Talent, how have his talents helped the team and others communicate? Has the employee been a mentor or facilitator for others? If so, what benefits or outcomes have occurred? If the person is a Club in a leadership role, how have others benefited by her leadership? If the individual is a Spade and good at organizing, how have his talents contributed to efficient processes or team functioning? What is the impact of that individual's efforts?

Impact is not always easy to assess. To learn their impact, knowledge workers have to look for objective results and ask others for feedback. As a leader you can provide valuable information to employees on their impact. When you see the talents of employees in action, give them feedback on what you appreciate. Let them know the positive or even negative impact of their talents on the team and others.

Align Talents with Priority Business Needs

Aligning employee talents with business needs means employees must stay tuned to what's happening in the organization. Often the real work that needs to be done in an organization has no title or job description. More career opportunities lie inside the white spaces between functions than within a job description.

Encourage employees to consider strategic directions and imperatives. Cues to business needs can often be found on the company's Web site and in quarterly and annual reports to stockholders. Talk openly with employees about the direction your organization is taking so they can assess where their talents fit in.

Promote Networking with Peers

Encourage knowledge workers to cross-fertilize with others. Suggest they volunteer to help out for an hour here or there in another department. They can also talk to colleagues at gatherings and find out what they're doing. Knowledge workers love to network. Allow employees to look outside their own department for cross-functional opportunities that might be there. There may be team members working on issues that are right up their alley.

Turn Frustration into Opportunities

Advise employees to notice what upsets them, and take note of it. Problems are fertile ground for employee contributions. Frustrations also reveal interests and problems the employee might want to do something about. Encourage employees to consider how they can apply their talent to critical areas and they'll be less frustrated.

Proactively Contribute Ideas

Teach your employees to scan for relevant opportunities and encourage them to come to you with ideas. Help employees recognize high-need areas with big payback. Also alert them to projects that have low impact on the real priorities. But, most importantly, challenge employees to think about how their contributions can lower costs, improve efficiency and effectiveness, and increase customer satisfaction. When knowledge workers think this way they become more valuable in today's world.

Encourage Action and Risk Taking

To leverage their talents in new ways, employees have to take risks and get involved. If it helps, list all the potential projects individuals have discovered in one column. In the second column describe actions they might take to contribute. Then, ask them to identify and talk to leaders in the company who have a strong interest in solving these problems. Advise employees to define the outcome they can achieve and the steps they want to take to get there. Encourage them to shape their role and contribution on the project so they can deliver on their talents.

In current positions, help employees find ways to clear their plate of random projects—especially those not aligned with their talents. There may be ample opportunities within the employee's current role to use their talents more. Advise employees to look for opportunities right where they are and bring ideas to the table.

Remove Barriers to Success

Identify any obstacles the employee might encounter. Secure support for the employee to move in new directions and take on an expanded role. The more critical to business needs the project is, the more likely individuals are to gain support for what they are proposing.

Help Employees Take Charge

Knowledge workers must step into the driver's seat to leverage their talents. Nobody else can do this for them. Otherwise, it's like driving to work each day and saying to the boss, "What do you want me to do? I'll do whatever you want." This approach may work for lower-level jobs, but the more an individual wants to be promoted in this economy, the faster he or she needs to learn how to play the new game. Otherwise their services are seen as low value.

Advise Going the Extra Mile

"Why should I volunteer for more work?" the knowledge worker might ask. "I'm already putting in a full week and then some." The short answer is that doing the right work leads to jobs that are more right for you. When you're working on projects that interest you, you're going to have greater energy and enthusiasm. And you'll add significant value.

Stay True to What You Do!

Staying true to our talents requires discipline. It's more than a one-shot decision. There are many internal pulls and demands that drag employees away from what they do best. The following barriers can stymie employee development, performance, and job satisfaction. Recognize these barriers and address them.

Number 1: Undervaluing Their Talents

Oftentimes employees do not recognize their value and thus remain in a job that doesn't utilize their full capabilities. For example, a graphic designer who's great at designing innovative solutions might resign herself to doing routine work. She doesn't appreciate how valuable her talents are so she sticks with lower-level tasks and wonders, "Is that all there is?" Help employees recognize the true value they bring. Don't retain them in a position because you're reluctant to lose their valuable skills. Encourage them to rise to the level they are capable of achieving.

Number 2: Opting for the Wrong Job

Employees who do not have a good understanding of their talents—and weaknesses—often take jobs that are wrong for them. For example, an engineer I once worked with stepped into a management role even though he had no affinity or desire to manage people. He rationalized his true interests by saying, "I'm doing this for the sake of my career and for the benefit of the organization. This experience will make me well-rounded." Sometimes this is true. But taking a job you hate can also prove fatal to your career.

Help employees honestly assess their strengths and weaknesses before taking a new assignment that might not be right for them. Don't hesitate to share your perceptions. Encourage them to move in directions that are compatible with their strengths.

Number 3: Trying Too Hard to Please Others

Some knowledge workers suffer from the "disease to please" syndrome. I knew one man who came from a family of doctors.

So, naturally, he became a doctor. The trouble was he didn't really want to be a doctor. He wanted to be a sculptor.

In the workplace, employees may try to force-fit themselves into a position simply to please a boss or do what the organization needs. This works for a while but ultimately ends up being exhausting and demoralizing. Some degree of flexing is essential in organizational life, but not when it grates on the individual day in and day out.

Coach employees when they are obediently heading down a path that is simply not right for them. Encourage honesty and give them permission to make decisions that are right for them. In some cases, this may mean leaving the organization if there isn't a path available that fits their talents and your business needs.

Number 4: Letting a Job or Company Pull You Away from Your Talents

The classic case here is the entrepreneur who's gifted at launching and building new companies, but then gets locked into a managerial mode. His talents and desire lie in starting new ventures, not hanging around in meetings about policies and procedures that bore him. He may be mildly successful staying on with the company he's built—but he's happiest when he's getting a new venture off the ground. In a larger corporation, a manager may discover she's been promoted to a position that doesn't interest her. A superstar sales professional moves up to be a sales manager. Suddenly everyone is unhappy. Why? Because the new sales manager is doing her employees' job. This superstar doesn't want to let go of direct involvement in customer accounts. Recognize when a promotion is actually a "demotion"—when the person needs to go back to what they do best.

Whenever an individual assumes a new position on a team, help her look anew at the impact of her strengths in this new role. See what's different in this role and find ways to bring the employee's strengths to the job.

Number 5: Allowing Laggards to Linger

An individual on your team may tell others he's sick of his job and he "really wants to be doing something else." But the individual doesn't take the actions necessary to change anything. Whether it's talking to another department or working on a new project, the person doesn't take actions that will lead to a new position.

Over time, the desire for change can marinate in the individual's mind. He just thinks about it for too long, and eventually gives up. Scientific study of the brain confirms that the longer we do something, the more entrenched our neural pathways become. This isn't to say employees cannot change, but change will require more of a concerted effort. It's easy to get stuck in a rut; as time passes, it becomes increasingly difficult to abandon the familiar.

If you have employees who are biding their time, challenge them to move. Find ways to get them out of their comfort zone and encourage them to take risks. Let them know it's up to them to choose a different path. Until recently it was easier to "just stick it out for a few more months or years." But in the knowledge economy, low performers won't be able to survive in most organizations. Today, knowledge workers are compelled to keep moving forward. If employees don't make decisions and stay on course, the decision is often made for them.

We're All Learning

We're all pioneers in this emerging entrepreneurial landscape. And we're barely one generation away from the compliant, obedient mandates of the past. No one is immune to the change.

Leaders are struggling as much as employees to find their rightful spot. You can't promise knowledge workers upward mobility or job security. But you can help them be viable in today's marketplace.

Encourage individuals to take responsibility for their careers and look for ways to align their talents with business needs. Help employees grow and develop in their specialty areas, leverage what they do best, and compensate for weaknesses that impede progress. With a talent focus, everyone has the opportunity and responsibility to make a difference. Staying rooted in your strengths is the best development plan.

KEY HIGHLIGHTS OF CHAPTER 10

- Legions of knowledge workers are still heading up a career ladder that no longer exists.

- Today there's no practical way to devise a three- to five-year let alone a ten-year corporate ladder to climb.

- The best career opportunities are more likely to arise when we are doing what we love.

- Some employees are just marking time. Don't allow laggards to linger.

- Help employees verbalize how their contribution lowers costs, improves efficiency and effectiveness, and increases customer satisfaction.

Chapter 11

Address Performance Issues

PERFORMANCE REVIEWS RANK at the top of the list as one of the most dreaded experiences in organizational life. Perhaps the clearest indication of how ineffectual performance reviews are is that everyone dreads them. Few managers or staff members look forward to these meetings. Leaders see them as a chore that must be done. Knowledge workers are anxious before their reviews, nervous during them, and eager to escape afterward.

This is a shame considering that performance reviews are one of the few times you can sit down with your employees and have a heart-to-heart talk about performance, talents, and how their skills and abilities can be leveraged to meet company initiatives and goals. That's an opportunity that should be embraced—not dreaded. And, research shows employees actually want *more*—not less—feedback from their bosses. So what's the problem? It's simple: we don't want to talk about the tough stuff.

Here are three approaches managers use in a performance review.

SOME TYPICAL PERFORMANCE REVIEWS:

THE SANDWICH TECHNIQUE: The manager feels obligated to give both positive and negative feedback. So the manager says, "There are some things you are doing well. . . ." (Employee waits for the shoe to drop.) "And there are some things you need to improve upon. . . ." (Sure enough, the shoe drops.)

THE DODGEBALL STRATEGY: The manager shifts responsibility for the review onto the employee. "Well, how do *you* think you did this year?" Any frustrations the manager might have are easily bypassed by this approach.

DROP-KICK SOLUTION: A manager waits until the review to share pent-up frustrations. "Here are all the things I've wanted to tell you all year—but didn't." The employee hears the bad news and goes into shock and resentment.

Stop Blaming the Forms

In many organizations, human resource personnel spend countless hours designing performance appraisal processes. And, every year, managers and employees alike complain that the forms are too long and that the processes are convoluted and do nothing to align employee talents to organizational goals. But forms and rating scales are not the problem. The problem is that organizations focus on the wrong thing. There is only one reason to have a performance review. And it's not to communicate whether the person is a 2, 4, or 6 on a scale of 7.

The only purpose for a performance review is to help employees *contribute their best*. Period. It's that basic. And what that requires is not new forms—but more candid conversations where both parties get honest about what's working and what's not. Rather than rating, ranking, and rationing out feedback, leaders need to sit on the same side of the table with employees and explore ways the individual can contribute their best. Forthright and honest communication is essential to achieving this goal. A talent-focused performance appraisal system encourages employees to reflect on both strengths and weaknesses. But the attention should be on minimizing weaknesses—*not* developing or overriding them. It's a subtle but gigantic shift in focus.

So, should you just ignore employee weaknesses? Absolutely not. Tough love with self and others is the key to leading a strengths-based approach. In performance discussions, your role is to be a strength coach for the employee. Your role is to give honest feedback, identify opportunities that leverage employee strengths, and focus on outcome and results. The knowledge worker should also play an active role. It's the employee's job to bring in opportunities, assess personal performance, and identify ways they can offer value.

Don't Ignore a Weakness

Talking about an employee's weaknesses is not fun, but necessary. Team members and coworkers quickly recognize one another's weaknesses. But the individual involved may not see the problem. It's difficult to tell an overzealous employee that the very strengths he brings to the table are also a major source of frustration for the rest of the team.

The employee might be missing a key strength that's critical to the job. Or one of their strengths might also be a weakness. The following shows how even a positive strength can flip into a negative if taken too far. A "persistent" project manager can become "stubborn" when pushed to make a decision. A "friendly" account representative can also be a "pushover" in response to customers' demands.

STRENGTH	*BECOMES*	WEAKNESS
Persistent		Stubborn
Easygoing		Pushover
Enthusiastic		Unrealistic
Reliable		Slow to change
Spontaneous		Inconsistent
Smart		Know-it-all
Likable		Conflict averse
Dynamic		Overbearing

For example, Julie was a manager who took pride in her organizational abilities. But her employee, Heather, was not as neat and orderly. Julie was always on Heather's case. Julie constantly made Heather feel like she was not measuring up. Tensions mounted until they had an honest, frank discussion about the situation. When Heather explained the difficulty of living up to Julie's standards, a breakthrough occurred. Julie realized that by other people's standards, Heather's office was just fine. Julie had taken her organizational abilities to an extreme. Once Julie listened to Heather's concerns and took responsibility for her part, she let go of her perfectionism and recognized the value of "good enough."

Be on the lookout for strengths in yourself or your employees that could morph into a weakness, particularly if it is alienating coworkers or customers.

Tackle the Tough Stuff

Imagine that you have a smart knowledge worker on your team who overwhelms customers with his technical jargon. Without feedback, this person is not going to be effective. As the leader, you must address this problem early and nip it in the bud. The following is an example of what you might say.

"Tom, you are very knowledgeable and savvy about our computer system. We rely on your expert advice and problem solving. However, your technical strength is a weakness in this situation. When you interact with customers, they don't understand the terms you use.

"Unfortunately customers end up feeling resentful and stupid. They want their problem fixed now—but they don't understand what you are saying. They're asking me for another resource they can work with.

"I'm sure this is not what you want! You've worked hard to develop your technical expertise and have a right to feel proud. What are your perspectives about the situation?

"Are you willing to address this situation and make a change? Let's find a way to leverage your technical expertise and improve customer communication."

Now let's look at the five steps involved in this message to the employee:

1. *Recognize employee strengths and also the flip side of this strength.*
   "You are very knowledgeable and savvy about our computer system. We rely on your expert advice and problem solving. However, your technical strength is a weakness in this situation. When you interact with customers, they don't understand the technical terms you use."

2. *Share the impact of employee's behavior on others.*
   "Unfortunately customers end up feeling resentful and stupid. They want their problem fixed now—but they don't understand what you are saying. They're asking me for another resource they can work with."

3. *Assume positive intent and reinforce the employee's strengths.*
"I'm sure this is not what you want! You've worked hard to develop technical expertise and you have a right to feel proud."

4. *Seek to understand the employee's perspective.*
"What are your perspectives?"

5. *Invite the employee to find a solution and take action.*
"Are you willing to address this situation and make a change? Let's find a way to leverage your technical expertise and improve customer communication."

Always recognize strengths when you address a weakness with an employee. Let the person know you want their abilities to shine. Offer advice about concrete actions the individual can take. When done effectively, strength feedback corrects the performance issue without invalidating the employee.

Find the Strength in a Weakness

If an employee is acting out or has an annoying trait, identify the flip side of this trait. Often a cynic cares deeply about the success of a program. And the controlling individual wants to ensure positive results. Find the positive motive buried beneath the negative behavior and it will be easier to talk about tough issues. Recognize the problem, but also look for positive intent. Help employees address their angst so they can step into their strengths.

Sometimes an employee doesn't want to deal with a weakness. The individual may be in denial about the problem and closed off to crucial feedback. Or the employee may be unaware of the issue. Your first step is to help the person recognize that there's a problem and accept responsibility for his part in it. Until this happens, you're not going to get very far.

The more senior an employee, the more likely it is that she needs to actively solicit feedback from others. Seasoned employees need to ask themselves:

- Do I routinely ask for feedback?
- Am I approachable?
- Am I willing to listen and accept others' perceptions?
- Do I ask for suggestions?
- Am I willing to initiate new behavior?

It's not easy to deal with the flip side of our strengths. But every strength that is taken too far is a weakness that can derail the employee, team performance, and the organization.

You can head off problems by helping employees choose work that's aligned with their strengths. This is more of a challenge with senior-level employees because organizations often give employees the message that they must sacrifice using their talents or being fulfilled in a position to move up or earn more.

Perhaps an employee would prefer advising and coaching instead of a decision-maker role. So, ideally the individual seeks out a staff position. If the employee likes to start new projects, you can help her avoid getting into a job where she is managing routine work. Ask employees to take responsibility and put themselves in positions that are aligned with their strengths.

Five Strategies to Manage a Weakness

Once an employee recognizes a weakness and wants to work on it, here are some useful strategies you can use.

Number 1: Provide Structure and Boundaries

Jerry is a relentless micromanager. He tries to delegate to others but then checks in hourly to see what progress is being made.

To compensate for this weakness, help Jerry develop a system that gives him boundaries and structure. Jerry can establish a new routine and meet with his staff once a week instead of peppering them with questions all day long. He can rely on weekly e-mail to pose important questions to department managers, instead of continuously drafting a new message. He can make notes and keep them in his pocket until the appropriate time in a meeting.

Advise employees about structures and boundaries that minimize their weaknesses. Maybe they need to develop a template for weekly reports or a standard form for staff meetings instead of creating the agenda from scratch. In short, craft strategies to modulate excessive behavior.

Number 2: Delegate to Others

Ask employees to find a partner or coworker with a complementary talent to bring balance to their leadership. Encourage knowledge workers to partner with staff members who are not like them. For instance, Ronald Reagan needed a get-it-done manager like James Baker to focus on the details.

Number 3: Use a Strength to Manage a Weakness

Employees can also use their best talents to address a weakness. For example, Will was responsible for managing others. He didn't have much experience as a manager. But he did have extensive experience as a researcher and analyzer. So, he decided to use his researcher brain to find the information he needed to manage people. In other words, he took his strong talent in research and applied it to remedy a weakness.

You may have an innovator who is responsible for managing a project. The project requires paying attention to lots of details. So you can ask this employee to look for "innovative ways" to manage the details.

This approach has untold benefits. Once employees draw upon their strengths, it's like having a springboard for success. They feel energized to tackle the task, project, or decision that they might have avoided or performed poorly. Now they are seeing this responsibility through new eyes.

Number 4: Use a Talent Just a Little Bit More

We all have talents we do moderately well. Ask employees to use one of their moderate talents just a little more to improve the situation. As a spontaneous type, I'm good at addressing immediate issues. I realize however that my spontaneity can cause problems. I like to go with the flow—but sometimes this leads me in the wrong direction. If I spend just a bit more time on planning, but not to the point where I become a planner type, the rest of my activities and work life go much smoother. A little bit of planning goes a long way to improving my overall performance.

Number 5: Slow Down and Take Smaller Steps

When employees are faced with a big challenge that's out of their talent area, teach them to slow down. Ramona worked in the marketing department. Each time she met with her Web master, Mike, she felt anxious and out of sorts. Technology was not her "thing." She didn't understand it or like it. She liked to make fast decisions and get things done. But the meetings with Mike were way over her head.

Ramona shared this problem with her manager. Together, they developed a plan to address the situation. Ramona adopted a behavior uncharacteristic of her. She slowed down during the appointment times. And she wrote down the directions instead of trying to keep all this information in her head. As she took smaller steps forward, she started to learn more of the technical language and catch on more quickly. Remind employees to slow down when they are not in their talent area.

The key to managing any weakness is to get creative about possible solutions. Ask, "How can we manage this weakness with a minimum of effort so you can focus on your strengths?" See how many inventive ways you can find to manage a weakness. Then you and employees can focus on the good stuff you want to achieve.

Succeed with Core Competencies

Now let's look at how a strengths-focused approach applies when you are using a competency model of development. Competency models identify the core skills required for a job. Many organizations have already defined the competencies for various jobs in their company. Employees can be very good in some, or all, of the competencies required in their job.

The benefit of a competency model is that it gives leaders a tool to objectively say whether the employee is "high or low" in a critical skill needed for the job. Essentially you don't have to wonder what skills the job requires. They are spelled out for you.

The best ways to work with key competencies is to help employees align their talents with job competencies and manage areas where they have weaknesses. Here are the steps involved:

- First, identify the competencies or skills required in a specific job. Again, your organization may already have identified a set of competencies for different jobs.
- Ask employees to reflect on their talents and identify the competencies they are naturally good at doing.
- Next, identify areas where the employee does not have natural talents for a core competency. Decide if these areas are a priority and critical to this person's performance.

- Finally, develop a plan to leverage the employee's strengths and minimize weaknesses. Make sure all the competencies are met but do so in a way that honors the individual's best talents.

Ensure Key Competencies Are Achieved

The following shows how June and her director used her talents to meet core competencies. June is a new manager and she has a strong Heart Talent and is savvy with people. In her job there are four key competencies required:

1. Manage customer relationships
2. Sell the vision
3. Develop employees
4. Set strategic direction

As a Heart, she is confident in her ability to manage customer relationships, sell the vision to others, and develop employees. However, she is low in Club talents and not confident in her ability to establish strategic direction. She has never developed a strategic plan and she is new to this organization. Right now, June wants to use her Heart talents to develop good customer relationships and get her struggling team up and running in the same direction.

The strategy for her group was developed earlier. So in the immediate future, June does not need to create a strategy. However, both June and her manager recognize that strategic planning is an area of weakness. The question is, How does June establish strategic direction for her unit when this is a weak area for her? She does not want to distract herself from the more immediate Heart work that needs to be done with customers and her team. Following are some ways June and her manager can minimize this weakness and still get the job done.

SUMMARY OF JUNE'S JOB COMPETENCIES

1. Manage Customer Relationships: HEART TALENT
   - Understand customer circumstances and needs
   - Maintain customer trust
   - Take action to meet customer needs
   - High Strength: managing customer relationships

2. Sell the Vision: HEART TALENT
   - Advocate organizational strategy
   - Energize teams and business partners to take action
   - Use the vision in day-to-day activities
   - High Strength: selling the vision and gaining commitment

3. Develop Employees: HEART TALENT
   - Assess key strengths and development opportunities
   - Create a learning culture
   - Recognize and reward employees
   - High Strength: excellent relationships with employees

4. Establish Strategic Direction: CLUB TALENT
   - Organize information and data
   - Develop key strategies and tactics
   - Take action to execute the plan
   - Low Strength: low interest and talent in this area

These are the competencies required, and an assessment of her strengths. June and her manager developed the following ideas together to minimize her weakness in strategic direction.

PARTNER WITH OTHERS. June might team up with a mentor who is exceptionally strong in strategic planning and jointly tackle the job of strategic planning.

USE A TALENT A BIT MORE. June is a moderate reader. But she needs to learn about the business. If she reads a little more each week about the industry and environment, she will be better equipped to think about strategic issues for her business unit.

ADD STRUCTURE. June could use tutorial workbooks on strategy. Her manager can provide June with a basic template with specific tasks outlined and ask her to simply fill in the template.

USE A STRENGTH TO MINIMIZE THIS WEAKNESS. June can use her relationship skills to lead a focus group and conduct one-on-one interviews with key customers to gather marketplace data. Then she could get help to integrate this data into the actual plan.

DELEGATE THE TASK. Her manager might ask June to delegate the responsibility for strategic planning to a staff person or someone better qualified to lead this effort.

Challenge Yourself

When you meet with employees for a performance discussion, dive in. Be courageous. Get honest. Tackle the tough stuff head-on and find creative ways to bring out the best in employees. Ideally, you and the employees will leave these meetings feeling energized, more connected, and enthusiastic about what's possible.

KEY HIGHLIGHTS OF CHAPTER 11

- A good performance review includes talking about tough stuff.
- Always recognize strengths when you address a weakness.
- For every weakness, there's a complementary strength.
- For every strength, there's a complementary weakness.
- Find creative ways to manage a weakness so it doesn't detract from strengths.

Chapter 12

Build Trust to Succeed

IT'S ESTIMATED THAT up to 50 percent of time in an organization is wasted on lack of trust. That statistic is not hard to imagine if you consider all the time spent on infighting, gossip, and conflicts in most organizations. However, take a minute to ask yourself what area in your department would radically improve in terms of performance and results if you built greater trust? Do you have two key individuals at war? Are members of your team struggling to work with another department? Do you need more trust from higher-ups in order to further your goals?

As a leader, you can't afford to ignore trust issues. Trust is like the air we breathe—we don't notice it until it goes bad. Trust is the invisible glue that makes great teamwork and performance possible.

In low-trust situations, employees spend half their time defending themselves, documenting their decisions and actions, and watching their backsides. Lack of trust is the root cause of many failed partnerships, derailed projects, and employee turnover.

Trust Is Good Business

Trust is the knowledge worker's most valuable currency. High-trust relationships enable them to recruit others, influence change, and contribute their talents. Without trust, it doesn't matter how talented the individual is—their contribution is limited. When there's little or no trust, others won't share information, engage their services, or use their expertise in meaningful ways.

In high-trust relationships knowledge workers are able to:

- Communicate easily
- Be creative
- Take risks
- Address the real issues
- Learn from mistakes

In low-trust relationships employees often:

- Suspect the worst
- Waste time on rumors
- Hesitate to act
- Avoid each other
- Hide mistakes

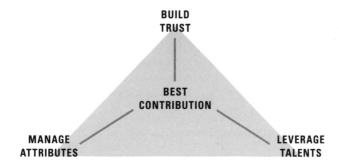

Building trust is at the top of the Play to Your Strengths talent system. Basically trust overrides all else. The degree of trust that exists among individuals, bosses, team members, and customers directly impacts business results. High-trust relationships allow individuals to contribute their best to the organization.

Don't Assume Trust Is Present

Trust is not a given in organizational life. Knowledge workers have to earn it, and that's often an uphill battle. In a Harris Poll of 23,000 U.S. employees working full-time in key industries responded on the topic of trust in the workplace:

- 15 percent said they worked in a high trust environment.
- 17 percent said their organization fostered open communication and differing opinions.
- 20 percent said they felt fully trusted by the organization.
- 13 percent said they had high-trust, cooperative work relationships with other groups and departments.

As you see from this data, trust is not easy to come by. With busy schedules, short deadlines, and scant communication, it's easy for trust issues to arise. And employees feel they have enough to do without having to deal with trust issues!

Learning how to build trust is one of the most valuable skills you can pass on to knowledge workers. Without this know-how, it's a hit-or-miss proposition as to whether employees will be able to address the real issues impeding their progress.

What Exactly Is Trust Anyway?

Trust is a degree of certainty that those you depend on will meet your expectation. Trust is feeling confident you can rely on yourself, another person, or a product you use. *All* economic activity requires trusting others to deliver on their promises. No exchange of any kind happens without some level of trust.

The 5 Trust Factors

Trust is multidimensional. From the research and literature available on the subject of trust, I've distilled five basic trust factors. Trust factors are behaviors that ensure trust. Rarely do we have all five trust factors present in one relationship.

1. *Competence:* I trust your knowledge and expertise.
2. *Commitment:* I trust that you do what you say you will do.
3. *Conflict:* I trust you to resolve any conflicts that arise.
4. *Communication:* I trust you to tell me what I need to know in a timely manner.
5. *Caring:* I trust that you will look out for my interests.

We may trust a person in one of these areas, but not another. For instance, you may trust that a colleague or subordinate cares about you as a person—but the individual may not be technically competent. However, we don't have to trust a coworker in all five trust factors to have a great working relationship with that individual. What's important is that we can trust the person in one or more of five areas. We especially want to trust the person in areas where we must rely upon them for something. Equally important is that we recognize when we can trust the person—and when we can't. Trust requires discernment.

Get acquainted with the five trust factors and also share them with your team. Knowing the trust factors helps employees talk specifically about what they need from each other. Now let's look at each of the five trust factors in the work setting.

The Competence Trust Factor

When you delegate work to employees, you consider whether they have the knowledge and skills to do the job. If you trust their competence, you rely on them to make good decisions and proceed wisely. Essentially, you trust their knowledge and expertise and rely on their competency. In the work setting, competence trust is the basis for work that transpires between individuals.

Employees must trust that each of their competencies work well together. When employees don't trust one another's competence, they won't rely on the judgment or skill of other team members.

All the trust-building exercises in the world won't overcome problems related to competency issues. Competency is one of the most fundamental trust factors in a work setting. When competency trust is lacking, elaborate networks evolve, designed to neutralize or bypass these weak links. The result is always further erosion of trust.

In bureaucratic-type organizations, competence can be a burning issue. If you are quick to hire people and slow to fire them, competence issues may not be addressed. If you keep poor performers onboard, everyone in the organization is negatively impacted. Trust can fall to the lowest of levels simply because of a competency issue. Especially among knowledge workers, professional competence is a key factor that builds trust.

Talent Types Perceive Trust Differently

To complicate matters, each talent type perceives the trust factors differently. For instance, a Heart Talent views "competency" as the ability to read a situation and respond with emotional intelligence. For a Club Talent, "competency" is seen as grasping the larger vision. The Spade Talent sees "competency" as being accurate and thorough. And the Diamond sees "competency" as the ability to be creative.

A Spade Talent who can't think outside the box might be perceived by the Diamond Talent as being incompetent. Or you might have a Heart Talent who connects well with people, but the Spade Talent thinks he's incompetent because he can't remember details. Competency is in the mind of the beholder. It's easy to misjudge each other and assume incompetence when we're looking through different lenses. Each talent type judges the other from his or her own competency bias and finds the other lacking.

Help employees recognize that "competency issues" may be related to having different perspectives and priorities. Ask employees to move beyond judging and to find common ground around what is important for the business. Work to meet the real priorities versus judging each other's competency.

Acknowledge that it's important for individuals to be competent in their positions. Address problems and concerns about individual competence. Nothing destroys trust more than allowing poor performance to continue.

The Commitment Trust Factor

Commitment means knowing that we can trust other people to do what they said they would do. The commitment trust factor is important among knowledge workers because their work is so interdependent. The employee may not be able to complete a report until he receives important data from another person. If the other individual is constantly late or fails to deliver this data, trust is broken. Even in small ways, trust is damaged when employees say they will attend a meeting and fail to show up.

It's critical for leaders to engender commitment trust. Ideally employees believe the leader means what he or she says and will follow through. It's easy to make pronouncements. But everyone watches to see whether there is action. New programs without ongoing commitment are seen as "le program du jour."

As a leader you must set a high standard for yourself and employees. Routinely ask yourself and employees these questions: Do you keep your commitments? Do you follow through? Are you good to your word? Do you expect others to follow through? Perception contributes to others' reality. Do you encourage individuals on your team to keep commitments to each other? If they make a commitment, do they follow up every time or are they inconsistent? If an employee promises to deliver a report but it is a week late, do you ask the question, "What happened?" and say, "I thought we had an agreement?" Do employees confront you and each other when promises are over-looked or broken? Holding each other accountable increases the degree of follow-through and commitment to agreements. Every level needs to be held accountable to their word. Trust is a two-way street. Employees won't keep commitments if they think you're not going to stick with *your* commitments.

Talent Types Perceive Commitment Trust Factor Differently
Spade Talents are naturally good at commitment. Spades like to make agreements and stick to them. And they expect others to do the same. Follow-through is a key Spade strength. Spades write down agreements, clarify them, and take action. The other talent types can view commitment very differently. For instance, if the Heart says she will be at a meeting that starts at 3:00, you can count on the Heart being there, but not necessarily at 3:00. The Heart feels fully committed because she plans to attend the meeting. But the Spade who has been waiting for ten minutes might feel, "I can never count on you!"

A Diamond whose funding is cut may feel that the Club leader who canceled the funds is not committed. The Club leader sees himself as totally committed—but to a different vision. Like-wise, the Club Talent may feel the Diamond is not committed to her vision because the Diamond questions the research behind the program. But the Diamond is totally committed to the pro-gram and simply pressing for ways to justify it to others. Com-mitment trust means different things to different talent types. Often more discussions and understanding is needed to clear up misperceptions about lack of commitment.

The Conflict Trust Factor

Trusting each other around conflict means: "I trust you to tell me when you have a problem. And if there is a problem, I know we can resolve the issues successfully." Dealing with conflict builds trust faster than any other activity. When knowledge workers know they can raise an issue and get the problem resolved, trust increases exponentially.

How well employees manage conflict is a critical trust factor. Do you trust employees to tell you when things go wrong? Or, do they skirt the issues, laying the seeds for problems and conflicts down the road? How well do you and your staff confront troubling issues and resolve them? Can employees work out their differences with each other? Can they count on you to notice and address unresolved conflict? When you and employees address a conflict situation, do you come out feeling good about the resolution and each other? If so, you're building trust and your team's ability to deliver high value.

When employees are confident that they can work through differences with each other, a climate of trust develops. Employees know they can come to you with a tough problem and you will not penalize them for it. They believe it's possible to work it out and come up with a solution. Employees are able to solve conflicts and move on without resentment.

Talent Types Perceive Conflict Trust Factor Differently

The talent types again have different perceptions about how to handle conflicts. In a conflict, Heart Talents don't want you to just solve the problem; they want you to recognize how they feel. If you address the problem but miss this key element, you may not regain the trust of a Heart Talent.

Club Talents look for a structural solution to the conflict. They may reorganize or put a new system in place. To a Club, if the solution is obvious, there's no need to talk it out among all the players. But employees feel overlooked rather than supported by this approach and continue to mistrust the Club.

The Spade talent wants to see a change happen immediately. This is the way they feel confident that the conflict is resolved. Concrete agreements and actions are evidence to a Spade that the problem has been addressed. Spades don't like to linger in messy conflict dynamics for long. They need closure and clarity to trust that the issue is resolved.

Diamonds see the conflict from every angle and can argue both sides of the fence. Others may not trust the Diamond Talent because they don't know where she stands on the issues. Diamonds can take either side. Because of this multifaceted view of the situation, the Diamond may be seen as untrustworthy.

Resolving conflicts among the talent types requires understanding what is important to each person. What's important to one type is very unimportant to another talent type. Respect for these differences goes a long way toward resolving conflicts.

The Communication Trust Factor

Communication is an issue in every company. Many trust issues are erroneously labeled communication issues. Communication Trust means the individual can be trusted to share important information that is helpful to others in a consistent and timely manner. In other words, team members trust each other to share vital information and keep them informed. With good communication between employees and leaders, there are no unexpected surprises. Individuals trust each other to convey important information and keep them informed about what they need to know.

Ask yourself, "Do you and others on your team share information that's important? Do employees tell you what you need to know? Do you give employees timely information? Can others rely on you to keep them informed? Can you rely on employees not to blind-side you?" Basically trust is built when individuals feel like they have the information they need to be successful.

No one likes surprises caused by lack of communication. Lynn was a Diamond manager in an IT department for a major medical device company. She was in charge of improving the phone system, and she was making great progress. But her major business unit customer, Brad, was a Spade talent, and he hadn't heard a word from her since the project began. Lynn felt great about the changes she was making. But unwittingly she lost her customer's trust.

Frequent, honest communication builds trust. If you sense that you need to communicate with an employee, a customer, or whomever, chances are, you're right! Pick up the phone or jump on your e-mail and do it. It's better to risk overcommunicating rather than undercommunicating. Your ability to build and maintain trust is at stake. Teach employees the value of communication by setting an example. Be specific about the information you might need. Encourage knowledge workers to do the same.

Talent Types and the Communication Trust Factor
Different talent types require different types of communication to build trust. Brad was a Spade talent. It was unthinkable to him to have a week go by and not know hear from Lynn about how the project was going. However, as a Diamond talent, Lynn was lost in her creative endeavor, confident that her innovative approach would wow the customer. Calling him was simply not on her mind. But Brad was a Spade and needed to have an update.

A Heart Talent wants to hear about people issues impacting the success of a project. But a Spade Talent might communicate project details but neglect to tell the Heart Talent that four people on the project are looking for a new job! The Heart feels,

"I just can't count on you to tell me what I need to know." A Club Talent wants clarity but the Diamond is still considering ten different options and spinning scenarios in her head. The Club sees the Diamond as confused and doesn't trust her.

Miscommunication is often the result of different expectations of the four talent types. Don't assume because it's not important to you that it isn't to others. Encourage employees to clarify the information they need to know. Making assumptions about communication is dangerous. The Heart waits for everyone to agree on a decision. She gains consensus, but lets her boss down by missing the deadline. Somehow we never get communication right. With talent differences, we're like ships passing in the night. Take time to clarify communication needs, understand what's expected, and improve communication trust.

The Caring Trust Factor

Letting others know that you care is a vital trust-building factor. If a knowledge worker on your team thinks that you don't like her, it's hard to forge an effective, high-trust relationship with that person. Communicating that you care about employees can be as simple as offering a warm hello to them in the morning. A gruff and abrupt response creates problems if it is seen as uncaring.

One of the first statements used to describe a new boss or new employees is the phrase, "Oh, I think he's nice." "Nice," while sometimes having a trite connotation, is important. It immediately conveys that you think the other person will be easy to work with and that she will be a caring person who responds to others.

Although the desire may be unspoken, knowledge workers want to know that they are cared about as a person. Employees want to work with bosses and peers who show they care and are willing to watch out for them. No one fully trusts a backstabber or egocentric leader.

Caring means recognizing the impact your behavior has on others. Do individuals in your group take time to show they care? Are thank-you notes sent when projects succeed? Do employees consider the effects of their actions? When knowledge workers believe that others care about them, they more readily honor requests.

The leader who takes a personal interest in each employee raises everyone's chances for achievement. Caring does not mean ignoring problems. Sometimes the greatest care you can give is to confront a situation. When caring about others is the norm, employees feel encouraged to do their best. If any member of the team feels left out, everyone is affected. Taking time to care about employees brings care in return. Employees watch out for leaders who care about them and put forth extra effort.

Talent Types Perceive the Care Trust Factor Differently

All employees want to feel cared about and know they are important. However, each of the talent types perceive that you care based on different behaviors.

A Club will want you to care about his big idea. Show a Club you care by being interested in his vision and endeavors. In like manner, Diamond Talents want you to care about their creative projects. You can show you care about the Diamond by taking time to brainstorm possibilities. If you are a Spade and don't like to brainstorm, then just listen to the Diamond Talent as she shares her creative ideas. For a Heart, you can show you care by being interested in her well-being. Heart Talents are often burned-out from caring for others. Take time to listen and let them unburden. Give a Heart permission to take a break and let go of everyone else's problem. Show a Spade you care by following through with your promises. This lets the Spade know that he is important to you. When you promise a Spade something, do it. If things change, care enough to let the Spade know right away.

Each of the talent types perceives "care" differently. Don't assume you can throw a Friday lunch and everyone will feel cared for. Take time to consider what each person needs and care enough to give it to them. Set the example and send the message that caring about others is important.

Use Trust Factor Language in Conversations

Teach employees the five factors of trust. Encourage them to talk explicitly about what they need from each other using the trust factors as a tool for communicating. A human resources person might let you know she needs "more timely communication." Another employee might tell team members he wants more "commitment and follow-through." Using the language of trust help employees ask for what they need from each other.

With talent differences at play, there are many opportunities for misunderstandings to arise. Promote two-way conversation versus e-mails. Nothing fuels conflict more than flaming e-mails. Advise employees not to jump to conclusions. Eighty percent of the time, the other person does not mean to let us down. Broken trust is often unintentional. Direct communication is the best way to build trust. Encourage knowledge workers to deal openly with trust issues. When trust is restored, other issues resolve themselves.

KEY HIGHLIGHTS FROM CHAPTER 12

- Roughly 50 percent of time in an organization is wasted on activities related to lack of trust.
- The five trust factors help you communicate precisely about trust issues and clarify what's needed.
- Very few individuals can be trusted in all five trust factors. Discernment helps us know when to trust.
- Every action we take either increases or diminishes trust.
- The more trust we have, the more likely others are to rely on our services.

Chapter 13

Conflict—Call It Off

CONFLICTS ARISE WHEN different talent types clash. A Spade Talent who wants perfection may collide with a Heart Talent who values relationships. A Club Talent who's driving for results annoys a Diamond Talent who wants to innovate.

Today's marketplace is competitive. There is too much at stake to allow employee conflicts to continue unabated. Knowledge workers are intricately connected and must collaborate up, down, and across the organization to achieve results. Conflict and mistrust are the enemies of performance and lead to costly delays. When problems erupt and employees can't move past them, you, as a manager, must step in and mediate. Your involvement in these situations is the single biggest deterrent to ongoing bickering and strife.

Talent Differences Cause Tension

Tensions are bound to arise when employees work together. It's part of life. However, conflict can happen more frequently among knowledge workers. Their intelligence, skills, and education make them more apt to think that they see the whole picture, when, in fact, all their perceptions are filtered through the bias of their particular talent type. You can head off problems by being alert to the following issues.

Potential Conflicts for Diamonds

Diamonds can annoy peers—especially Spades, when they intrude on an orderly process and insist on changing it. Diamonds, as well as other types, intrude on Spade territory and demand changes. Often they do this at the last minute. The Diamond Talent may not be aware of how frustrating this behavior is to Spades. Unexpected changes, combined with insensitivity to employees, can create tensions. This problem is especially difficult when the Diamond is working with employees who are at a lower level on the corporate ladder. The employees don't feel free to challenge the Diamond but they are frustrated by all the disruptions. Resentments start to brew and soon they boil over.

Alert Diamonds of the need to plan ahead and stay involved as others work to implement their great idea. Ask them to stay connected and attuned to administrative and service personnel so they can hear the early rumblings. Encourage them to take action early to ward off these conflicts.

Potential Conflicts for Hearts

Hearts are the most alert to conflicts in the environment. They know immediately when tensions are high. Others go to the Hearts with their problems and vent. But Heart Talents can get enmeshed in conflicts and issues that are not theirs to address. Sometimes Hearts get so involved, they take sides and champion the victim's cause. Hearts need to become aware of personal and work boundaries and recognize which issues are not theirs to address. Others can't learn to stand on their own two feet when Hearts do their dirty work. Also, a Heart type can easily be offended by an off-handed comment and carry around feelings of resentment without addressing it openly. Be aware of these smoldering feelings and help Heart Talents set boundaries and tackle issues directly with others.

Potential Conflicts for Clubs

Clubs can get into trouble when they are too quick to make decisions that impact others or fail to involve them in the change process. Clubs are sometimes astonished by others' strong reactions. Clubs cannot comprehend why anyone would object—especially when a decision is the right thing to do. The resulting conflict simply doesn't make any sense to them. Unwittingly, the Club has usurped another's authority and overlooked that person's right to have a say. Now the Club has a swarming hornet's nest around his head. Help Club Talents anticipate and prevent these types of conflicts. Ask Clubs to go "overboard," from their perspective, to check in and keep colleagues informed.

Potential Conflicts for Spades

Spades get a bad rap because they are the ones who see all the problems. They worry because they have to implement the ideas. But Spades can become thorns in the side of the team because they keep bringing up the problems no one else wants to address. Other team members want to have fun creating and developing the project, but the Spade keeps bring them back to earth—and soon everyone is frustrated. It's not long before they don't want the Spade person around. For Spade Talents it's hard to go with the flow and let things emerge. Spades are focused on order and efficiency—not flow. You can help Spade Talents realize there's a right time and place for them to share their concerns. Let them know that sometimes it's okay to sit back and relax—or more likely, make to-do lists in their heads. Also, help Spades with the presentation of their ideas. "That will never work" may be true—but it's hard for others to hear.

Talk about Stress Points
Talk openly about these natural tension points with your team and discuss the challenges of working together. By doing so, you name the "elephant in the room" and let employees know they're not alone. As a general principle, if you *sense* tension among employees or between an individual and yourself, you're probably not imagining things. Bring things out in the open by addressing the situation. Recognize hot spots and take preventative action so problems are avoided.

How and When to Get Involved
Conflicts are natural and to be expected. When you learn of a conflict or observe one, realize that you have a role to play. You must intervene if the situation does not improve. The worst thing you can do is to allow conflict to continue unchecked. When you get involved in employee conflicts, realize you can step in gradually. There are layers of involvement options—and the first is surprisingly simple.

Level 1: Notice the Problem
When there is a conflict among employees, you can simply notice it. Go to the individuals and say something. Simply commenting on the problem goes a long ways toward resolving it. When knowledge workers are not getting along, you can say:

- I notice that you aren't speaking to one another.
- This meeting seems flat. You're both quiet. What's going on?
- I sense there's tension between you and Jeff. Is this true?

Many times all you have to do is notice the conflict. This alone lets employees know there's a problem that needs to be addressed. This level of attention encourages employees to take initiative and address the issue.

Level 2: Talk Directly to the Individuals Involved

At this level, you go beyond noticing and talk separately to the parties involved. You want to find out what is going on, so ask them to talk. Once each person has shared her or his perspectives in private with you, you encourage the individuals to address the situation. And, of course, you're there to give them ideas and support if they need it. You leave it up to the individuals involved to address the situation in whatever way works for them.

Level 3: Bring the Warring Parties Together

If the previous steps don't work, you need to move up to the third level of involvement and bring the parties together. At this level you are a facilitator working to help the two parties fix the problem. In these conversations, you make sure the weaker party is given as much power to negotiate as the stronger party. Your job is to be a neutral third party who helps the employees at odds share their perceptions, acknowledge their part in the conflict, and agree on actions to move ahead.

Level 4: Take Action to Remedy the Situation

It isn't always possible to solve conflicts. Sometimes no matter what you do, there is no solution. The tensions and differences are just too deep. When this is the case, you need to take things in your own hands and remedy the situation. You can move an employee into another position, assign different duties, ask someone to leave—and in some way eliminate the conflict by taking action.

Reduce Conflict Between Different Talent Types

Here are some actions individuals can take to reduce conflicts with different talent types.

REDUCE CONFLICT WITH A SPADE

- Take time to understand the barriers Spades are facing.
- Work together to identify problem-solving actions.
- Be careful not to overload them with too much work.
- Make sure to appreciate their efforts.

REDUCE CONFLICT WITH A DIAMOND

- Support and acknowledge their bright ideas.
- Ask questions and respect their witty responses.
- Be interested in their projects and don't laugh at wacky ideas.
- Avoid blame; support learning from mistakes.

REDUCE CONFLICT WITH A CLUB

- Ask about their vision of what could be.
- Be brief and get to the point.
- Don't get bogged down in details.
- Know what you want and don't waste their time.

REDUCE CONFLICT WITH A HEART

- Take time to connect and engage in social conversation.
- Listen and respect their intuitions and gut perceptions.
- Welcome their insights about people and relationships.
- Don't be harsh and critical with them.
- Recognize they are thin-skinned, and tread lightly.

When faced with conflicts, you may think to yourself, "This is hopeless. There's nothing I can do about this." Yet often, it's possible to turn these situations around. Getting things back on track is a matter of clearing the air and gaining commitment to actions going forward. Employees basically want to trust each other and get along. It makes their work life easier and more enjoyable. But sometimes they need your help to do it.

At a hospital in Northern Colorado, the doctors and the nursing staff were at one another's throats. The nurses thought the doctors were rude and disrespectful. The nurses felt that they were being ignored, mistreated, and placed under unnecessary pressure. In short, they blamed the doctors for making their work lives miserable. The nurses also felt they had no right to speak up about the situation. In the medical staff pecking order, the doctors were on the highest rung. But the nurses were ready to bolt if things didn't change. And the hospital was on the verge of a staffing shortage that could have affected patient care.

To address this crisis, we held a meeting involving all participants and leveled the playing field. The location itself was neutral. We placed the chairs in a large circle to eliminate some of the power differences. By avoiding a face-to-face seating arrangement, we diminished the air of confrontation. During this session, everyone had the opportunity to address one another by first name. No titles were allowed.

Individuals had the opportunity to speak up and were given equal time to air their grievances. The nurses saw the doctors as poor planners, rushing about and prompting others to do the same. They also felt that the doctors treated them as work objects and showed them little respect. When the nurses finished talking, the doctors were silent and stunned.

The doctors also had some grievances and shared these openly. They felt the nurses were unresponsive. And they didn't like the preferential treatment they felt some of the doctors received from the nurses. Simply airing these differences and making sure that each side felt it was heard greatly diffused the situation. It was a tough conversation and the feelings ran high.

At the end of the session the doctors and nurses committed to a new way of working together. The nurses agreed to speak up and do so respectfully instead of grumbling to one another. And the doctors agreed to kinder interactions with the nurses and better coordination around schedules and logistics. After this session and airing of issues, internal teamwork greatly improved.

Make It Safe to Address Issues

In your role as conflict facilitator, it helps to have a road map to follow. The following steps will help guide you through the process. If you think you might get in over your head, call in a seasoned coach to guide you. Start the meeting by reminding employees that most offenses are unintentional. Employee perceptions can become reality all too quickly. As the session progresses, probe for what each side wants and needs.

Identify Shared Goals

Discover areas where both sides have a vested interest. Build on these areas. Look for similarities and shared agendas. Let employees know that they don't have to like each other to work well together. The foundation for trust is being able to count on others to do what they say.

Acknowledge Concerns and Move On

Continually recognize knowledge worker's feelings and perceptions. In these conversations especially, employees like to feel validated. Also, encourage individuals to move on once the issues are aired. You can say, "I think I understand your perspectives and views. Now what would you like to see happen? What actions are you willing to take to improve this situation?"

Don't Try to Fix the Past

The only reason to talk about the past is to let it go. It is next to impossible to gain agreement about the facts, so don't dwell on it. Stick to employee behaviors, perceptions, and feelings. Once concerns are shared, the question becomes, "What are you willing to do now?" Invite participants to move on and begin anew.

Follow Up and Stay Involved

Afterward, follow up and monitor their progress. If necessary, suggest additional course corrections. Invite employees to share what's working better, and what still isn't working. Encourage ongoing communication and progress reports. With practice, it becomes easier to address the issues and nip them in the bud.

Action Steps to Resolve Conflicts

Here are the steps to address conflicts between warring parties:

Initiate a conversation with the employees involved. Say to them, "I'm concerned about you and Sharon. It looks like you're not getting along. Is this correct?" Invite them to meet with you jointly by saying, "Are you willing to talk with this person directly if I'm involved as the facilitator? I think it's important to do this."

Find a neutral place to hold the meeting. Start the meeting by describing what you see. Share your concerns and talk about what's at stake if the conflict continues.

Set ground rules. For example, you can say, "I'd like to have everything that's said here, stay here." Then ask the individuals to take turns sharing their opinions and perceptions. You will need to revisit the critical incident(s) that happened. Ask each person to share his or her perceptions and views on the situation freely. Reflect and summarize what you hear from each party—without judgment.

Once employee's perceptions and feelings are aired, suggest a shared goal. You can say, "This project requires your combined efforts and talents. How do you want to proceed?"

Ask for specific behaviors each wants from the other. Say, "Sharon, what specifically would you like from Jeff?" and vice versa. Once you have three to five behaviors, ask for commitment to these behaviors. Write down the agreements.

Always follow up. Periodically ask employees, "How are you doing? What is going well? What changes have you made?" Intervene again if necessary. Your interest and support helps employees keep going in the right direction. Simply put, to deal with conflicts, you must get the players in the room, get the issues on the table, get agreement about what's needed—and get on with it!

As a leader, like it or not, dealing with conflicts is part of your job. Without your help, employee frustrations burn up too many productive hours. So take heart and get involved. It's very rewarding when you have a win in this area. Your involvement gets employees back on track and doing meaningful work together.

KEY HIGHLIGHTS FROM CHAPTER 13

- Conflicts arise when different talent types feel disrespected by each other.
- The leader needs to get involved when employee conflicts escalate.
- You can reduce conflicts by simply noticing the problem.
- When facilitating conflict resolution, help employees discover a shared goal.
- To solve conflicts, get the players in the room, get the issues on the table, get agreement to take action—and get on with it.

Chapter 14

Know the Score!

ACCORDING TO JACK WELCH, former CEO of General Electric, lack of feedback in the workplace is one of the biggest roadblocks to a company's success. In bureaucratic-type organizations in particular, people are often afraid to be candid. Welch advocates developing a culture that encourages and rewards honest feedback. "You'll reinforce the behaviors that you reward," he says. "If you reward candor, you'll get it."

In any game, there is a score. It's no different in business. Ultimately, your score is the value of what you deliver. To learn the value of your contribution, you must ask the customer. Feedback is the only way to find out whether you're on target.

In our Play to Your Strengths Talent System, contribution is at the center of the model. Employee contributions are not what they deliver—but what the customer receives. To ensure customer satisfaction, employees must ask for feedback on their deliverables. Success is in the eye of the customer.

The Value of Strength Feedback

The goal of feedback is to help employees make their best contribution. Ideally feedback is proactive instead of reactive. Feedback doesn't work if it's only about shortcomings, frustrations, and weaknesses. Don't wait for review time to use this valuable tool! Once a problem arises, it may be too late to fix it. With feedback, you want employees to discover what's working right and keep going in that direction. Sometimes the only clue they have that something is amiss is a comment offered by a caring customer or employee.

Curiously, the word *feedback* is tainted by misconception. Employees don't look forward to feedback, and many have a negative experience with it. Sometimes, it may seem easier to just sweep your concerns under the rug and hope that problems will work out on their own. But you will let employees down if you skirt the real issues.

Feedback Is a Powerful Tool

Encourage employees to use strength feedback as a growth-enhancing tool to support individual and project goals. A capable employee I coached named Praveen decided to develop his "advocacy" skills. He was a caring Heart Talent, but he wanted to develop more Club abilities in order to champion a new initiative. He used feedback to help him succeed. Here's how he did it.

First Praveen clarified what he wanted to achieve. He wrote down the reasons he wanted to develop advocacy skills:

- Implement a new information technology system
- Secure funding and resources for the new system
- Persuade coworkers to pilot the project system
- Secure upper-management support for the system
- Gain confidence in his ability to champion change initiatives

To get started on this goal he asked three individuals to give him strength feedback on his current skills and also recommend new skills that would help him become a successful advocate. Over the next twelve months, Praveen worked to develop advocacy skills and champion the system. Throughout he asked for feedback about what was working and what was needed. Eventually, Praveen gained support for the new initiative. He also developed strong advocacy skills in the process. Praveen used feedback proactively to achieve his goal.

Teams Benefit from Strength Feedback

A team can also use strength feedback to achieve their goals. One team I worked with decided they were too "Spade-like" and task oriented. In team meetings they talked primarily about tactics. Their customers wanted innovation—but team members felt that they were stuck in a rut. So they set out to become more Diamond-like and innovative in their approach. First they took time to clarify the changes they wanted to make. The following is their list of desired changes:

DO LESS	DO MORE
Talk about tactics	Learn new approaches
Solve immediate issues	Plan for the future
Rely on their experience	Bring in expert resources
React to problems	Explore innovative ideas
Respond to requests	Offer solutions to customers

They developed a simple survey and rated themselves on each of these items. Six months later they reassessed themselves on these goals and asked customers for feedback as well. Each person looked for ways they could be more Diamond-like and creative in response to customer requests. As a team they brought in a creativity expert to teach them brainstorming techniques. Collectively they worked together to create new solutions for their customers. Their meetings switched from being exclusively tactical to making plans for the future.

Defining clear goals and asking for strength feedback helped this team keep their feet to the fire and achieve their goals. After a few months, customers were singing their praises and grateful for the new solutions being offered. Over time these knowledge workers became strategic partners with their customers instead of just service providers.

Help your team use strength feedback as a tool to stay focused on personal and team goals. Ongoing feedback is encouraging as well as instructive. Employees initiate change faster when others notice their progress. Essentially feedback is a caring way to help others deliver their best. However, not all feedback is helpful.

Give Strength Feedback

The type of feedback that's sorely needed is strength feedback. The goal of all strength feedback is to help individuals deliver their personal best. It's shared without anger or blame. Strength feedback is vitally important. Knowledge workers are dealing with important projects that involve lots of people and big dollars. They must learn quickly when others have a problem. And they are motivated and encouraged by hearing what they did well.

Employees cringe when they hear the words, "I'd like to give you some feedback." They know it's not going to be positive. In fact, they're probably going to be told to correct something they've doing. Often feedback is unsolicited, meaning the individual has not asked for it. And there are many occasions when feedback is delivered badly.

BAD Feedback

Some feedback is BAD feedback. BAD feedback is peppered with statements like, "You screwed up," "You're wrong," "I can't believe you did that," and "You had better get it straight." BAD feedback is full of blame, anger, and demand for change.

Blaming—you ruined it!
Angry—I'm mad at you.
Demanding—You better change this now.

BAD feedback puts employees on alert. This type of feedback creates negative reactions and defensiveness. Meanwhile, the real problem goes unresolved. Bad feedback usually takes place when an individual is emotionally out of balance. Ideally it's important to wait and cool down before addressing hot issues.

Create a Feedback-Rich Culture

In a strengths-focused culture, every employee is encouraged to give strength feedback. Strength feedback shines the light on employee talents and also recognizes weaknesses that hinder progress. In no way is strength feedback supposed to let employees off the hook. Suggestions and advice are freely given to help individuals make their best contribution.

Make Feedback Routine

Make strength feedback a part of your daily management practice. You don't have to wait for something important to take place. Notice what's working well. For example, at the end of a staff meeting, invite employees to say what they appreciated about the meeting. Ask team members what went well and what could go better. Invite comments on what they liked and also ways to improve the meeting next time.

When you finish a project or task, hold a debriefing session. Ask questions such as, "What went well?" "Who contributed what?" "How did team members benefit from one another's talents?" "What can we do better next time?"

Leaders Benefit from Feedback

As a leader, you need to invite feedback from employees. When Ed Koch was mayor of New York he used to ask the people on the street, "How am I doing?" Some people thought this was a publicity stunt. Others thought the mayor was simply being chatty. But he was using these exchanges to gather feedback about his performance. Koch found that the person on the street could be quite candid. His approach gave a new definition to "management by walking around." As a leader, if you want to know how you're doing, you need to ask—and not be afraid of the candid feedback that may result.

Ask Employees for Feedback

Ask your employees, "How am I doing?" Say to them, "I'd like to get your opinion on how I handled this situation." Or, "Could you help me? I'd like to hear your views on . . ." You can ask pointed questions such as, "How am I doing on communication?" "How am I doing in terms of delegating tasks?" "What issues am I not addressing that need to be addressed?" "What are three ways I can improve when delegating assignments?" "What's the one thing I could do to lead team meetings more effectively?" Ask individuals to be specific and suggest changes they'd like to see.

If you receive BAD feedback, keep probing and asking questions. Wait for the anger to die down and follow up with a discussion about the person's real concerns. Take some time to clarify and learn more. There is useful information buried within the negativity. Stay as objective as possible and extract the valid elements from an otherwise negative message. As you increase your capacity to receive feedback, employees will speak up sooner about their concerns.

Set the Example for Others

The more you ask for strength feedback, the more you encourage knowledge workers to also ask for feedback. Giving feedback to the leader is difficult for most employees. If employees can give you feedback, then it's easier for them to give it to one another.

TIPS FOR GIVING FEEDBACK

Use these rules when giving feedback about a weakness.

1. Ask permission to give feedback.
2. Give feedback on specific behaviors, not generalities.
3. Always assume positive intent.
4. Share the impact of the others' behaviors on yourself and the business.
5. Don't give the person more feedback than he or she can handle.
6. Make sure the feedback process is a two-way street.
7. Do not give feedback when you are emotionally upset.

Use Different Feedback Methods

You can use one or more of these methods to promote feedback among individuals and team members:

360-DEGREE FEEDBACK: Ideal for soliciting feedback from multiple partners and stakeholders.

TWO-WAY FEEDBACK: Great for encouraging dialogue between the manger and employees and even with customers.

TEAM FEEDBACK—OR "THE SANDBOX" METHOD: Ideal for helping team members to be successful with key projects.

SPOT FEEDBACK: Provides individuals with useful feedback for a specific situation.

FEED FORWARD PROCESS: Helps individuals plan actions to achieve a future goal.

360-Degree Feedback Process

Providing 360-degree feedback is when you seek input on your performance from the people who work with you. In this method individuals ask their boss, peers, subordinates, and customers to provide input and feedback on their performance. Many 360s are done online and the results can be seen immediately.

A 360-degree feedback process is extremely useful if it's done right. Ideally, you should encourage employees to talk directly with the people who gave them the feedback. Trouble can happen when this communication loop is not closed. Encouraging two-way communication about results completes the feedback cycle and clears up misunderstandings. With interaction and dialogue added to 360-degree reports, employees feel encouraged to continue what works and to add new behaviors as needed.

Two-Way Feedback

The two-way feedback process is new and coming into its own in many companies. In a performance appraisal meeting, two-way feedback is shared between the employee and the manager. First the employee receives feedback from the manager. Then the employee gives feedback to the manager. This method invites both participants to talk openly about ways to improve performance. Leaders seek input from employees about ways they can be more effective as a leader. And the employees seek feedback from the manager on their strengths and areas that need improvement.

Team Feedback—or "the Sandbox" Method

Team Feedback—what I've nicknamed "the Sandbox," is done in a team setting. Any individual on the team can ask for the group's time and receive feedback on a project. The individual invites others into his or her "organizational sandbox" to offer ideas on how to proceed. The person in the sandbox explains a specific challenge to the group and asks of the following questions: "What am I doing right? What could I do better? What actions do you recommend?" The team then goes to work on these questions. The individual who asked the questions leaves the room or listens but does not interfere. Once the team has developed a set of recommendations, they present their ideas to the individual. This person listens to the feedback and takes notes. No interaction or interruptions are allowed at this time. At the end of the feedback, the individual may ask questions and clarify the ideas. Then he or she thanks the team for their advice and returns to the group as a participant. The Sandbox method of feedback helps break down boundaries and turf protection.

Spot Feedback

Spot Feedback is literally done on the spot. The knowledge worker asks the manager or a colleague for spot feedback. If two individuals are in a meeting and one is giving a presentation, the presenter might ask her colleague to give her feedback after the presentation. Spot feedback can be used when employees are struggling with a personnel issue, want advice about interactions with a boss, or when preparing for a customer meeting. Basically, the person says, "Can you give me some feedback on this specific topic? I'd like some help wording this proposal . . .

or feedback on my timing, or some ideas about implementation." Spot feedback takes five to fifteen minutes at most. It's done on the spot. It is also referred to as "just in time" feedback.

Feed Forward Method

The Feed Forward Method is focused on the future. The way it works is that a knowledge worker shares an idea she is considering. The idea might be about a future project, product, or service. Next she describes her vision and what she wants to achieve. The other individuals listen and ask questions to understand her vision. Then she asks the group, "What talents do I need to bring forward to succeed with this new endeavor? What do I need to watch out for? What actions do you recommend I take to achieve this goal?" Others advise her about strategies she can use to succeed with her vision. All the feedback is phrased as "You could do this or you could do that." The Feed forward method is a powerful way to put fuel behind someone's vision and give the person a jump-start. You can use the feed forward method in meetings and group settings.

At its best, feedback is a mirror that allows us to see what we cannot see ourselves. We are never too seasoned or high up to not profit from others' feedback and support. Feedback goes hand in hand with goal setting to help employees achieve results. Honest, insightful feedback helps employees contribute their best. It's time to take this underutilized tool off the self and put it to use.

KEY HIGHLIGHTS FROM CHAPTER 14

- The purpose of feedback is to help individuals contribute their personal best.
- Soliciting feedback is the only way to learn the true value of our contribution.
- A strengths-focused culture is rich in feedback.
- Learning to freely give and receive feedback takes some getting used to.
- When a leader asks for feedback, employees will follow the example.

INNOVATORS   MOTIVATORS   ACTIVATORS   IMPLEMENTORS

Part 4

Take the Lead

Chapter 15

Play Your Trump Wisely

PROFESSIONAL SPORTS OFFER an effective model for how to lead knowledge workers. Major sport franchises understand how to seek, recruit, and manage talent. Their scouts are always out looking for the best players. At the start of each season, coaches and recruiters scramble to find the most effective lineup and have the best substitutes ready so their team can compete and win.

The climate within organizations today should be more like a sports franchise. A coach strives to bring out the best in the players. The coach values high performers, holds onto them, and sees these individuals as assets. Meanwhile, he works hard to bring all the players—not just the "A" players—up to speed.

You'll never see a football coach running onto the field and taking the snap from the center. The coach always stays on the sidelines and works *on* the game, not *in* the game. Leaders today need to emulate this practice. Ideally, you should strive for group synergy instead of relying on star performers to carry the day. The wise leader knows that great team results require more than one star player.

Become a Strength Coach

One of the crucial roles you can play as a leader of knowledge workers is that of a "strength coach." Strength coaching helps individuals recognize what they do best, develop their talents, and align these talents with business needs. Your role is to help your employees see opportunities, take charge, and contribute in a meaningful way. As a strength coach you realize that listening and asking questions is more valuable than offering advice. You focus on employees' concerns and you also provide perspective and guidance at key points. In coaching conversations you expand employees' awareness of their talents and success pattern. You help them manage over- and underused talents and attributes. You also advise them on ways to build trust with team members and individuals connected to their projects. The goal is optimum contribution and employee growth.

Watch from the Sidelines

As a coach you work from the sidelines. You're constantly assessing ways to develop the individual's talents, optimize their natural attributes, and compensate for missing talents. The Play to Your Strengths coaching program has the following coaching goals.

We strive to help individuals:

1. Leverage their best strengths.
2. Recognize and develop emerging strengths.
3. Manage over- and underused talents.
4. Identify opportunities to further use their talents.
5. Communicate their value to others.

Your role is similar. You want to help employees bring their best talents to the organization.

You Are Both a Manager and a Coach

As a leader, you are both a "manager" and a "coach." In the management role you are responsible for business goals, managing performance, and administering work assignments. As a coach, you develop employees' talents, help them learn from mistakes, and empower them to take charge.

COACH ROLE	MANAGER ROLE
Develop abilities	Set goals and outcomes
Leverage talents	Communicate priorities
Foster learning	Hold others accountable
Manage weaknesses	Measure progress
Find opportunities	Manage performance

Sometimes the roles of manager and coach collide. As a manager, you may have to remove or reassign an employee to a new area. As a coach, you help employees understand what is needed, why it's important, and help clarify actions they can take.

Like the coach on the side of the field, you don't jump into the project. But you keep a constant tab on how the game is progressing. You recognize individual and team successes. You celebrate achievements so employees are encouraged to jump into the next project. You notice when there is activity with few results and you call attention to this. You communicate the vision and priorities again and again and make sure actions are under way to achieve them.

Address Problems

In a coaching situation, you might have a talented employee, like Jason, who loves to take charge. Jason is a Club Talent and has no problem stepping up to the plate. But what do you do if Jason takes charge to a fault? He might make decisions so rapidly and so often that no one else has a say in the matter. Or perhaps you have a different employee who is highly motivated but wants all the credit?

Confronting these issues is not easy. For a Spade employee, a looming deadline might be problematic. They become short with others and difficult to work with. As a coach, your role is to help knowledge workers deliver their best. This means addressing both work projects and interpersonal glitches and finding ways to resolve them.

Recognize Your Coaching Strengths

You will be better at coaching in some areas than others. If you are a Diamond talent, you'll be good at asking questions and helping employees think. As a Club talent, you'll be able to bring clarity to messy situations and help individuals bring structure to them. If you're a Spade leader, you can help employees define practical actions that lead to results. And as a Heart talent you'll be adept at helping others address interpersonal dynamics and teamwork issues.

The following is a summary of the coaching strengths of each talent type:

- CLUB TALENTS help individuals clarify their vision and architect what's needed to ensure desired outcomes.
- DIAMOND TALENTS have a knack for asking employees just the right questions to help others see things from a new perspective.
- HEART TALENTS help individuals understand work relationships and build trust with others. They can suggest strategies to keep motivation high and relationships on track.
- SPADE TALENTS can offer individuals expert guidance on how to improve key processes. On a practical level they help

others think about what's needed to help a project cross the finish line.

Each leader offers different coaching expertise and has a set of biases because of their own unique talents. You're probably strong in one or two talents and low in at least one of the talents. If you can't provide the insights that employees need, recommend others who can coach them in this area. You can also use questions to help the individual address this area. For instance, if Heart talents elude you, you can still help an employee who wants better cooperation from others by asking questions like:

- What can you do to increase cooperation and teamwork?
- How would you like to be treated by others on the team?
- What are your ideas on ways we can build greater trust?

As a coach, you work to leverage your talent strengths and compensate for any talent weakness.

Ask Great Coaching Questions

The most important skill of a good coach is asking questions. Taking the time to consider the right questions to ask is more helpful than just dictating answers that employees should follow. When momentum and progress are fading, you can ask:

- What do you feel you are doing right?
- Where are your challenges?
- What could be done better?
- What actions will you take to accomplish that?

Asking the right questions helps people think. The right question gets employees past their mental blocks and helps them gain new perspectives. The question "How can your talents contribute to a solution?" helps individuals focus on what they can do to support the larger goals. Most importantly, questions encourage ownership of the answers employees derive.

Asking good questions is an art. Most leaders are not trained in questioning and listening skills. Listening and questioning skills represent the very essence of coaching. If you need to, take a class, get feedback on your approach, and learn the skills required to be a good coach. If asking questions does not come naturally, you can write out the questions and then schedule time for coaching.

As a coach you do not want to take on the problem or be the "answer person." Your job is to listen and allow the other person to talk. It's very tempting to say, "Here is what I would do," or "You should try this." Or even worse, "You should have said or done this." A coach listens 80 percent of the time and talks 20 percent of the time.

Listening Skills Help You Stay on Track

Over time, employees will realize that by listening they are providing a useful, productive service to the other person. It takes time and experience to recognize that listening and asking questions works. Once the person has shared fully, they might ask for advice and perspective. This is where your talent expertise can help. However, as a coach you should avoid giving this too early in the meeting.

Good coaching is about creating space and the opportunity for the other person to explore and uncover ways to look at an issue. It is not intended as a way to dump problems in another's lap and be given an easy solution. Coaching questions invite the other person to think more broadly and creatively about the issue and possible solutions.

Encourage Reflection

As a coach your primary role is to encourage reflection. Asking penetrating questions helps employees reflect on their role in situations. But it requires restraint and discipline. In the beginning, you may feel that the time spent in coaching is not worthwhile given the urgency of immediate deadlines that you and your staff face. But over time, you'll see that coaching pays off royally. Good coaching helps knowledge workers learn how to think and make better decisions.

Follow Guidelines for Coaching

The following guidelines will help you become a solid strength coach:

Schedule a specific time for the coaching. Meet even when you feel you don't need to. Regular meetings are the building block of successful coaching. Don't let weeks go by without checking in or communicate only when there are problems. Identify ways to stay connected, talk frequently, and keep abreast of what's going on.

Coach each person differently. One size doesn't fit all. Every employee is unique. Ideally, you tailor your approach to the unique needs of each person. Some employees respond well to dialogue and interaction. Others want clear direction. Consider the experience level and personality style of each employee and adapt your coaching methods accordingly.

Promote independence. A team member who is dependent on your advice is not benefiting from your coaching. Increased accountability and initiative are the key indicators of successful coaching. Listen, ask questions, and place more responsibility for decisions with the employee. Avoid being the answer person.

Develop thinking skills. Your primary role as a strength coach is to teach your employees to think. You want to ensure that the right decisions are being made even when you're not around. Your role is to teach knowledge workers how to analyze problems and make decisions that produce high-quality results. The quality of your questions determines the quality of their thinking.

Broaden employee perspectives. You want to broaden the playing field and open the individual's mind to new ways of seeing the problem. Encourage employees to take a step back and look at the situation again. Ultimately, broader perspectives produce better solutions. Many times you will help individuals reframe a situation and see it completely differently.

Make a commitment and follow up. Before each meeting is over, agree on actions the employee will take before the next meeting. Encourage employees to try something new—like making a difficult decision, giving a presentation, or tackling a controversial issue. Hold employees accountable for actions. Ask them to do homework and share what they learn.

Keep confidences. Confidentiality is implicit. All conversations among peers are confidential and not to be shared outside. Take special care not to reveal confidences.

Have fun. It's great fun to learn and grow. Enjoy your time together. Celebrate employees' successes, appreciate their strengths, and notice how they thrive on your encouragement.

Launch Peer Coaching

You can also encourage knowledge workers to be strength coaches for each other. The coaching role doesn't have to be solely on your shoulders. Often, team members can have outstanding advice for one another. Encourage team members to pair up and become coaching partners. Peer coaching is also a powerful way to break down cross-functional barriers and promote teamwork.

Opportune Times for Coaching

Opportune times to coach individuals are at the beginning and end of a project. You can help knowledge workers set up projects successfully and reflect on key learnings and what went well. At the initiation of a project, encourage individuals to discover and use their talents. After the project is completed ask them to reflect on their performance, what they learned, and what they will do differently next time.

Coach Before a Project Launch

Here are coaching questions you can ask at the start of a project:

- What are the goals of this project?
- Specifically what will success look like?
- What talents do you bring to this project? Where can your talents add value?
- What parts of the project might be challenging? What do you need to watch out for?
- What other talent types are needed to ensure success?
- How do you plan to set up yourself, others, and the project for success?
- What actions will you take?

Coach to Debrief Project Performance

Immediately after a project is finished is another excellent time to coach employees. The insights and learnings from these coaching sessions are fresh and useful. The following are strength-coaching questions you can ask to help knowledge workers grow and learn from their experiences:

- What went well on this project? What could have gone better?
- What tasks and activities did you especially enjoy working on?
- Where did your talents shine while working on the project?
- What are some of the challenges you faced?
- How did you address these? What did you learn?
- What contribution did you make?
- Where do you believe you've made a difference?
- What feedback did you receive from others?
- What will you do differently next time?

Coaching knowledge workers helps you let go of control and turn over responsibility to employees. As a coach, you can easily support success and help employees learn from mistakes. Coaching is an essential tool for leaders who want to develop and maximize the talents of knowledge workers.

KEY HIGHLIGHTS FROM CHAPTER 15

- The leader is both a coach and a manager. Sometimes these two roles collide.
- Your talents impact your coaching abilities and the guidance you offer.
- The role of a coach is to help employees shine.
- Coach your employees before and after major projects.
- Asking questions and listening attentively are the primary tools of a strength coach.

Chapter 16

Coach Others to Win

WHEN COACHING Michael Jordan, coach Phil Jackson observed that Jordan, who led Chicago to six championships in the 1990s, was a highly skilled player. But what really set him apart and made him an *extraordinary* player was the fact that Jordan was willing to be coached.

Many athletes are gifted. They need to be to play at a professional level. But Michael Jordan became a superstar because he didn't rely on talent alone—he was willing to be coached. He embraced the challenges Jackson gave to him. He came to practices with an open mind. He listened to and learned from Jackson. Undoubtedly, he also helped his coach to be a better coach.

The Employee Has a Role in Coaching

As a leader it's your job to help your employees recognize and utilize their talents. However, employees also have a responsibility in the process. You can teach individuals how to be good recipients of coaching. Basically you do this by communicating their responsibilities and encouraging them to ask for what they need. For strength coaching to work it must be a two-way street. To benefit from coaching, the knowledge worker needs to be:

- Willing to be challenged and open to learning
- Receptive to feedback and accept personal responsibility
- Action-oriented and follow through on advice for improvement

During coaching, expect employees to take an active role, and start by discovering knowledge workers' talents. Always be alert for even small ways the employee wants to contribute.

Bring Out the Best in Others

A good coach continually assesses the status of the game, what needs to be accomplished, and which players on the roster can best meet the challenge. The coach has an in-depth understanding of each player and what he or she contributes to the team. The coach also realizes that in the next quarter, the team lineup may need to be reshuffled to win the game. A wise leader knows how to bring out the best in each player and the team.

It's one thing for employees to know their talents, but it's often a challenge to find the proper outlet. The Play to Your Strengths coaching process will help you align employee talents with business needs.

Prepare for Coaching

Think of the employee and ask yourself the following:

- In what situations has the individual performed well?
- What motivates this employee day-to-day and in the long term?
- What opportunities might be a good fit with the individual's talents?

- What are some of the employee's weaknesses or blind spots? How are these areas impacting this individual's contribution to the team or organization?

You can also invite the employee to complete the following prework on their goals and desired outcomes of the coaching process. Hand out the following questions ahead of time and discuss them when you meet.

COACHING PREWORK FOR EMPLOYEE

1. My goals for the coaching process are:
2. Outcomes I want over the next three months:
3. How I learn best is:
4. Qualities I'm looking for in a coach:
5. What I want from a coach:

Develop a Coaching Contract

In your first meeting, develop a coaching contract. Basically you want to jointly identify the goals you want to achieve. You also want to establish time frames, specific dates, and length of meetings. At this time, share any expectations you have of the coaching process. Talk about what you want from each other and write it down. A coaching contract helps you get off to a good start.

SAMPLE COACHING CONTRACT

- Our goals:
- The coaching process:
- Dates:
- Length of meetings:
- Expectations:
- Coach agrees to:
- Employee agrees to:

Learn the 5 Step Coaching Process

The following five-step process helps you align employee talents with business priorities. Following this process helps you ask the right questions, stay focused, and ensure the best results. The strength-coaching process is simple and straightforward. Each of the steps is sequential. Do not skip a step, as this causes problems later on. Start the coaching process by getting in sync, then move on to explore and work with strength areas. Next, find opportunities to use employee strengths more broadly, and finally, determine the actions that are necessary to achieve the goals.

Step 1: Get in Sync

In the first step you get in sync with the employee and identify the coaching goals. This step makes the rest of the process more effective.

EXPLORE OPPORTUNITIES

- What is your current role? (Ask this if it isn't clear.)
- Where are you satisfied and dissatisfied with your current responsibilities?

EXPLORE GOALS

- What do you want to achieve with coaching?
- What specific goals do you have?

EXPLORE EXPECTATIONS

- What would you like from me as a coach?
- What can I expect from you in the coaching process?

Step 2: Explore Talents and Strengths

The goal of this step is to explore employee strengths. The employee may wish to develop new talents, manage the flip side of a talent, or learn more about his or her best talents. Together you and the employee explore strength areas. Also, tell the employee what you think she does well. Clearly describe her talents and her impact on others. Express your appreciation for this ability. It helps employees to see their talents through your eyes.

Foster self-awareness. Ask the employee to observe times during the week when he felt motivated and energized. Discuss these experiences. Identify key talents that emerged.

Help the individual clearly articulate her strengths. Remember, most employees don't recognize their strengths. Here are some questions you can ask regarding talent:

EXPLORE HOW TO USE TALENTS

- What are your best talents?
- Which talents are you using in your current job?

EXPLORE THE IMPACT OF EMPLOYEE TALENTS

- How do your talents contribute to your success?
- Specifically, how do others benefit from your talents?

EXPLORE TALENT INTERESTS

- Which talents would you like to use more?
- Is there a hidden talent you'd like to develop?

EXPLORE TALENT WEAKNESSES

- Do you have a talent weakness that hinders your success in your role?
- Do you use one of your talents to excess? If so, what happens?
- Do you have a talent you'd like to develop more?

As you discuss talents, also identify job requirements that might be pulling the individual away from his natural talents.

Help the employee become aware of her special strengths. Also help employees identify and address weaknesses. Don't waste time trying to improve a basic weakness. You'll accomplish more by helping team members mine their strengths. Help employees recognize weaknesses and acknowledge when they're getting in the way of performance. Then determine how to manage them or how you can delegate these responsibilities to others who are better suited to handle them.

Step 3: Align Talents with Business Needs

Match projects to employee strengths. Identify projects that align with the individual's strengths and interests. Brainstorm an ideal project. Ask the employee to identify a project that "has her name written all over it." Invite the employee to describe this project in detail. Ask, "What type of work is it?" "Who is working with you?" "What about this project excites and engages you?"

Help team members identify ways to use their strengths on projects that interest them. Brainstorm assignments that capitalize on the person's unique ability to persuade, organize, or create, and then identify work assignments that will use these talent strengths. In this step you jointly explore ways to enhance the knowledge worker's contribution to the organization. Ideally, by the end of this step you and the employee have defined opportunity areas. You can facilitate the discussion by asking:

- What are some key issues, opportunities, and business problems the organization needs to address?
- What projects interest you?
- What issues attract you and energize you?
- Which problem or opportunity has "your name on it"?
- How might your talents contribute to a solution?
- Where else might you use your talents?

Give your input and advice on how the employee can contribute. Ask the employee to link her strengths with areas for growth for the business.

Step 4: Know How Talents Contribute to the Bottom Line
Help employees describe the benefits that their talents can bring to a project or position. The following are positive results the employee might impact:

- Decrease costs
- Improve efficiency
- Improve staff retention
- Increase response time
- Decrease operational expenses
- Increase sales
- Improve collections

- Increase revenue
- Produce more billable hours
- Reduce labor costs
- Minimize a risk
- Add revenue streams
- Increase market share
- Improve customer satisfaction
- Reduce cycle time

This list of benefits is reprinted with permission from Jill Konrath, from the book *Selling to Big Companies*.

Ask the individual to complete the following statement: *I can help this organization succeed by using my best talents (name them) to achieve (be specific about results).*

Step 5: Plan Actions
In this step, specific plans are made to take action. You and the employee decide who does what and by when to commit to this plan of action. You can offer additional resources and support, but the main responsibility for implementation lies with the employee.

Following are the questions you can ask to define the actions needed:

- What actions will you take?
- Who can help us?

These are action strategies you can help the employee use to leverage his or her talents:

- Reshape current role
- Manage time better
- Find a mentor with expertise in a specific area
- Access the talents of others to moderate a weakness
- Take a class to learn a new skill
- Lead a project to gain experience
- Seek feedback from others on how to use strengths

Clarify your willingness to support the employee and clarify the action steps by asking:

- What help do you need from others or myself?
- What resources and support do you want?

Without this process to follow, you might start saying, "Do this" and "Do that" instead of asking good coaching questions. Strength coaching is an ongoing process. It can involve spot coaching in the moment, as opportunities unfold. Simply ask, "Are you open to some quick feedback?" On-the-spot coaching, added to weekly or monthly meetings, can work wonders.

Keep Your Eye on Success

As a strength coach you ensure that projects and employees are on track. Be sure to acknowledge what's working well, check progress, and ensure results. Be available to help employees debrief, learn from mistakes, and celebrate successes.

Realize Employees May Have the Talent—but Not the Interest
When someone is burned-out in an area, be sensitive to the situation. Don't ask the individual to keep at it, months and even years after the thrill is gone. See if you can find an apprentice or ask them to mentor others and pass on their skills. Allow individuals to grow in areas where they display interest and enthusiasm. Recognize the need for a change early before valuable employees depart, leaving everyone befuddled.

The Benefits of Coaching
Strength coaching positions you as a resource for employees—not as someone who dictates how work should be accomplished. Employees see you as a partner who helps them discover the answers they need to be effective. Employees will become more independent, they'll make better decisions, and they won't be dependent on you to solve every problem. Strength coaching helps you develop and retain high-talent players and put their talents to use.

KEY HIGHLIGHTS FROM CHAPTER 16
- Strength coaching improves the individual's contribution.
- The employee needs to be willing to be coached.
- Listen and ask good questions to be a helpful coach.
- Don't pick up the problem and solve it for the employee.
- Help employees align their talents with business needs.

Chapter 17

Up the Ante!

IMPLEMENTING A COLLABORATIVE, strengths-focused culture is not easy. Here is how one leader succeeded with his division. Bill Gold was the vice president and chief medical officer of the Health Management Division at BlueCross BlueShield of Minnesota. Bill is a strong Club Talent and a visionary leader. As a physician Bill recognized the value of health prevention as the way to improve health care for members. So he launched several health improvement initiatives in his division. His vision aligned with the larger corporate vision "to make a healthy difference in member's lives."

Bill realized that achieving the vision would require a culture of teamwork and collaboration among divisional units. He started by communicating the vision to his leadership team and asking for their feedback. Leaders on the team told him, "Bill, you're driving down a road and we're in the back seat—but we can't see where you're going!" Bill's strength was his ability to create and hold a powerful vision. His weakness was adequately involving others in the vision.

With this feedback in hand, Bill set about making personal changes. And the team set to work on the vision in earnest. Team members realized that they didn't know much about one another's areas. Each person had a full plate, so the team spent little time together. They saw how their lack of synergy was permeating the entire division. They committed to working together and becoming more forthright with each other. They realized if change was going to happen—it had to start with them.

Do Things Differently

Top leaders started communicating more—and with greater candor. Each leader asked for feedback from team members and took time to recognize leadership strengths and weaknesses. They set leadership goals and clarified ways they could contribute to the larger vision. In staff meetings, leaders talked openly about successes, challenges, insights, and lessons learned. Gradually team members began to rely on each other, build greater trust, and synchronize their efforts. Instead of problems lingering below the surface, leaders addressed them head-on. They became advocates for each other and close-working colleagues. All the while, Bill stayed the course. His Club talent helped leaders stay on track. He never wavered and kept the vision foremost in everyone's mind.

The Coaching Breakthrough

A major breakthrough took place when top leaders started coaching each other. This turned out to be a stroke of genius that ultimately paved the way for greater collaboration. Each leader coached another member on the team. In these coaching sessions, individuals learned about each other's challenges, dreams, and aspirations. Coaching helped team members leverage their individual strengths, manage missing and overused strengths, and define actions they could take to meet business goals. Soon their trust and openness began to permeate the entire division and improve collaboration at every level.

Engage Employees
Leaders saw the need to engage all employees to make the vision a reality. They wanted to create leaders at every level, so they invited employees to sponsor activities and develop fun ways to encourage involvement. Quickly employees caught the spirit and ran with it. They tackled the culture, sponsored peer-coaching programs, and created positive ways to connect with one another. The culture slowly began to change and consistently move in the right direction.

Bill knew it would take years to build a collaborative culture. He believed that open communication and employee initiative was the only way to achieve the vision. Over the next four years the culture steadily grew and became more positive. Leaders kept delivering a consistent and unified message. Because their resolve was evident, employees at every level started to embrace the vision. The change was palpable.

Track Progress and Results

After four years, leaders felt the culture had changed for the better. But they were lacking real data. So as part of a wider corporate initiative, the division took part in a corporate survey to see if the progress was indeed real. When the results came back, the division's scores were at the top of the charts! Despite the potential for layoffs in this division, a whopping 81 percent of employees said they would encourage a friend to seek employment there.

80 percent said they were proud to work for the company.
75 percent reported that they enjoyed coming to work.

91 percent said they had a good relationship with their immediate supervisor.

74 percent believed that management heard and considered their ideas.

78 percent believed they had opportunities to utilize their strengths.

On average, most companies score at the 45 to 65 percent range on these same questions. These high scores were a direct result of leaders paying attention to the culture.

Learn from Experience

Recently I asked Bill to reflect on this five-year journey. In our meeting, I posed the following question: "Bill, what have you learned in this experience?"

He mused, "To change the culture, I had to change myself. I had to become more vulnerable. I also needed to become a better listener and invite others into the decision-making process. I learned that engaging employees was very important."

"What did you do to make believers out of employees?" I asked.

"We had to keep a consistent focus on the vision. It's easy for all of us to get distracted by the next new thing. We also asked employees to take personal responsibility. We kept asking, 'What can you do to improve teamwork and communication?' Their commitment was very important. We need leaders at every level—not just at the top."

"What changes do you see in the culture now?" I asked him.

He replied, "Today there's a lot less time spent on negative reactions and mistrust. Employees believe what they hear. They know how they fit into the bigger picture. There's more nurturing and support and less time spent venting at the water cooler.

Employees take charge and proactively use their talents. They have a greater sense of meaning and purpose in what they are doing."

"What about the vision?" I asked.

"I think it really helped to have specific projects to work on. We actually did something. We now have a better disease management program and a new Center for Prevention. Employees have a lot of pride and satisfaction in these accomplishments. They also feel greater recognition, respect, and appreciation for their efforts. With your help I learned that culture change must be linked to a driving business need. Having specific projects gave employees a reason to work together and collaborate on specific issues."

As our meeting closed I asked him, "Bill, what surprised you the most about this culture change process?

He frankly admitted, "I'm surprised it worked! It's actually different around here. The results are palpable and real. You can feel it when you walk in the door. This is very gratifying."

Don't Leave It to Chance

Creating a collaborative, strengths-focused culture takes work. The biggest barriers are prevailing attitudes and behaviors—or cultural barriers. Adopting a collaborative, strengths-focused culture sets the expectation that everyone is accountable. Strengths are recognized *and* problems are addressed. Greater trust and accountability help everyone rise to a new level of leadership. A strengths-focused culture isn't "make-nice" management. It's for leaders who want to tell the truth, build trust, and help employees maximize their talents.

Get Ready to Play

As a leader, you can implement a strength approach in many different ways. You can use these ideas to improve your personal leadership effectiveness, you can adopt a strengths-focused approach with your work team, and you can champion a collaborative, strengths-based culture throughout your entire division or organization.

At the individual level, any leader or employee can embrace a strength focus by discovering and leveraging her or his unique talents. At the team level, you can help team members recognize their individual talents and bring their collective abilities to bear on business initiatives. And at the divisional and organizational level, you can champion a strengths-focused culture and encourage employees to take initiative and use their talents fully.

At whatever level you choose to implement these ideas, use the guidelines presented on the following pages to help you get started.

Discover Your Strengths First

Begin with discovering your strengths. Take time to assess your talents and recognize your unique abilities as a leader. Ask yourself, "What kind of talents do I have? How do my talents help you contribute as a leader?"

If you are a Heart Talent, you're going to lead very differently than a Club Talent. All four talents inherently have a different impact. Ideally by now you see that you don't have to be like anyone else to succeed. The power of your leadership comes from claiming your authentic talents and leveraging your unique abilities.

Take time to reflect on your talents and clarify your value as a leader. If you're a Club talent, you bring clear vision and direction. As a Heart talent, you motivate others. If you're a Diamond talent, you inspire innovation. As a Spade talent, you leave no stone unturned to achieve the goal. Bravo to you all! Cherish these talents and make the most of them.

Share Strengths Principles with Employees

Continue by sharing the model and principles of a strengths-based approach with employees. Take twenty minutes in a staff meeting and talk about the Play to Your Strengths model (Chapter 3) and discuss the basic principles (Chapter 4). Employees will quickly catch on and apply these ideas to their experiences. Spend time talking about the idea of focusing on strengths. Ask employees, "What would we do differently if we focused on strengths?" and "How can we pay more attention to what's going right?"

Help Employee's Recognize and Appreciate Their Talents

Encourage team members to discover their talents. An easy way to get started is by asking individuals to take the Talent Assessment at *www.playtoyourstrengths.com* and talk about the pros and cons of their talent type. Also use the talent-focused activities provided in the appendix of this book with your team. It can take as little as twenty minutes to identify and share individual talents—and you'll have a great deal of fun. Give employees abundant feedback on their talents and help them find projects ideally suited to their abilities. Don't assume employees know their strengths. Take time to notice employees' strengths and give them feedback. Tell them where they add value to the organization. Your insights are enormously helpful to employees.

Implement a Strengths Focus with Your Team

The biggest return for your investment is using these ideas with your team. A team of individuals who know how to leverage their talents to achieve the vision is gold. Help team members recognize one another's talents. Teach your team the value of talent synergy and how to leverage one another's abilities. Promote peer coaching and talent handoffs. Don't leave team synergy to chance. Teach employees how to sync up and align their talents to achieve bigger goals.

Integrate a Strengths Approach with Ongoing Activities
Incorporate the strengths principles in your daily leadership practices. Use a strengths approach to address performance issues, develop employees, and coach individuals. There's practical information in Part 3 to help you create a shared vision, deal with conflicts, address performance issues, develop employees, and encourage feedback. It's all in here. Just open up a chapter, read the ideas, and put them to use. If you're going into a performance review, read the chapter on giving strength feedback and integrate these ideas into your review. Find easy ways to adopt these ideas as you go about your daily activities.

Play Your Best Hand
In *Play Your Best Hand*, you've learned about the new game of business and how to win *big* with knowledge workers. You know the nitty-gritty of how to discover your talents and how to leverage employees' talents as well.

The secret to success is appreciating everyone's talents. The more you do this—the more often you'll win. Focusing on strengths takes your leadership to the next level. Be sure to practice the basics so you get off to a good start. As you play, always remember the rules. And realize there are others around you playing a different game.

Ideally, you'll invite others to join you because it's more fun and rewarding that way. Simply apply these winning strategies, and you'll play many consecutive rounds. Once you get started, there's never a dull moment. The action is fun, fast, and action-packed. With this knowledge and an awareness of strengths—you're ready to go for the gold!

Play Your Best Hand was created exclusively for you by Faith Ralston and brought to you by the Knowledge Economy. I hope you enjoy playing!

KEY HIGHLIGHTS OF CHAPTER 17

- A climate of trust and openness helps employees contribute their best.
- Adopting a strengths-based culture makes it easier to set the expectation that everyone is accountable.
- Any leader or employee can embrace a strengths-focused culture by discovering and leveraging his or her unique talents.
- The biggest bang for your time is implementing these ideas with your team.
- A team of talented individuals who know how to leverage their talents is gold!

Appendix A

Play Your Best Hand Tool Kit

Tool 1: Discover Your Talents

1. What are your favorite projects or activities? At work? At home? In social situations?

   This question helps you spot areas where you're already using your talent. Remember, your talents show up everywhere you do.

2. What do you choose to do even when no one is paying you to do it? At home? At work?

   This question helps you identify the activities you gravitate toward.

3. What do others consistently ask you to do?

   This question helps you see how others already use your talents.

4. How do others describe you?

   This questions helps you recognize the unique talents you bring to every situation and interaction.

5. When do others get annoyed with you? *This question helps you see when you're overusing a talent.*

Tool 2: Create A Contribution Statement

A Contribution Statement helps you communicate your talents to others. Work is easy and fun when you're doing what you do best. Write your Contribution Statement by filling in the following:

- I love to do the following:
- Please call me when these problems and challenges arise:
- I can help you achieve these specific results:

Tool 3: Identify Your Success Pattern

Your top talents work together in a predictable pattern to achieve results. Complete these steps to identify your personal success pattern:

1. What are the five to seven talents you most enjoy using? Write each one on a note card.
2. Which talent is your "central" talent—or the one you enjoy dong the most? Place this talent in the center of the other talent cards.
3. What is the order in which you like to use your talents? Arrange the cards to show this order. Be creative. Place your "central" talent in the middle and place the other talents around it. Lay out the ideal sequence in which you like to use these five to seven talents.
4. How do you like to work and deploy your talents? Find a partner and describe how you like to work. Learn how your partner likes to work. Notice the differences and similarities.
5. What talents and steps are critical to your success?
6. What have you learned about your success pattern? What do you want others to know about your success pattern?

Tool 4: Recognize What Makes You Unique

Attributes are your style or unique way of being. To discover your attributes, answer the following questions. Also ask close friends and colleagues about your attributes—you will likely be surprised by what you learn. Recognize the value of your leadership attributes.

1. What three to five words best describe you?
2. How would you describe yourself to a person who does not know you?
3. When you work on a team, what attributes do you bring to the team? If you weren't involved, what would be missing from the team?
4. In your opinion, what is the one positive attribute that makes you distinctive and special?
5. What is the value that you bring to others because of this attribute? Be specific.

Tool 5: Leverage Your Best Talent

Assess whether your best talent is a Heart, Spade, Club, or Heart talent. Then identify the value you bring to others when you use this talent by answering the questions provided.

DIAMOND TALENTS PREFER TO:

- Think of innovative ideas
- Challenge the status quo
- Find hidden opportunities

SPADE TALENTS PREFER TO:

- Complete projects on time
- Manage the details
- Put out fires

HEART TALENTS PREFER TO:
- Build trust and teamwork
- Address conflicts and people issues
- Help others manage stress

CLUB TALENTS PREFER TO:
- Sponsor new initiatives
- Build useful alliances
- Advocate for change

KEY QUESTIONS TO ASK:
- How often do I use my talents now at work? Other places?
- What problems are solved when I use these talents?
- How can I let others know what I can contribute?

Tool 6: Manage a Weakness

Identify a weakness. Refer to the four talents on the previous page and pick the one you have the least interest in doing. Choose one of the following strategies to manage this talent and keep it from hindering your performance.

1. Partner with another: Who has a talent that complements one of your weaknesses?

2. Eliminate the task: What tasks could you stop doing?

3. Systematize your efforts: What habit, routine, or technology can help you manage this weakness?

4. Delegate to someone else: Who else could help you with this job or task?

5. Compensate with strength: How can you use your best talent to manage this weakness? (For example, if you are innovative but not good at details, you might find an "innovative" way to manage details.)

Tool 7: Give Strength Feedback

Think of an employee you would like to give feedback. Complete the questions that follow and write what you want to say to this person:

- I see, hear, feel this is happening . . .
- I assume you have these good intentions . . .
- Your strengths are . . .
- A flip side, or weakness, of this strength is . . .
- How your behavior or attitude impacts others and myself is . . . (describe both the positive and negative impact)
- What I'd like to see is . . .

Tool 8: Assess Trust in Self as Leader

All trust begins with self-trust. This assessment helps you identify the degree to which you trust yourself as a leader. Identify where you have high and low trust in yourself. Take actions to improve areas of low trust.

Communicate   As a leader I can count on myself to:

Share information

Low	1	2	3	4	5	High

Communicate openly

Low	1	2	3	4	5	High

Listen attentively

Low	1	2	3	4	5	High

Respond quickly

Low	1	2	3	4	5	High

Ensure two-way communication

Low	1	2	3	4	5	High

Competence   As a leader I can count on myself to:

Be talented and capable

Low	1	2	3	4	5	High

Use my talents wisely

Low	1	2	3	4	5	High

Act appropriately

Low	1	2	3	4	5	High

Make good decisions

Low	1	2	3	4	5	High

Share my expertise

Low	1	2	3	4	5	High

Commitment   As a leader I can count on myself to:

Do what I say

Low	1	2	3	4	5	High

Clarify expectations

Low	1	2	3	4	5	High

Keep promises to others

Low	1	2	3	4	5	High

Keep promises to myself

Low	1	2	3	4	5	High

Take a stand for what I believe

Low	1	2	3	4	5	High

Conflict   As a leader I can count on myself to:

Address tough issues

Low	1	2	3	4	5	High

Accept personal responsibility

Low	1	2	3	4	5	High

Do what's best for everyone

| Low | 1 | 2 | 3 | 4 | 5 | High |

Allow others to disagree

| Low | 1 | 2 | 3 | 4 | 5 | High |

Resolve conflicts

| Low | 1 | 2 | 3 | 4 | 5 | High |

Care As a leader I can count on myself to:

Enjoy time alone

| Low | 1 | 2 | 3 | 4 | 5 | High |

Appreciate who I am

| Low | 1 | 2 | 3 | 4 | 5 | High |

Take care of my own well-being

| Low | 1 | 2 | 3 | 4 | 5 | High |

Be aware of my own needs

| Low | 1 | 2 | 3 | 4 | 5 | High |

Receive help from others

| Low | 1 | 2 | 3 | 4 | 5 | High |

KEY LESSONS FROM SELF-ASSESSMENT

- I trust myself in these areas:
- I want to build greater trust with myself in these areas:
- Actions I plan to take are:

Appendix B

Great Resources

On Talents

Now Discover Your Strengths, by Marcus Buckingham and Donald Clifton (Free Press). This is a must-read for any consultant who wants to develop a strengths-based approach. It is an excellent book that stresses the importance of focusing on what's right.

Leverage Our Best, Ditch the Rest: The Coaching Secrets Top Executives Depend On, by Scott Blanchard and Madeleine Homan (William Morrow Press). This book has great tips aimed at helping individuals deliver their best. It encourages focus on what does work, and intolerance for what doesn't work. It's good for coaching individuals and challenging yourself to step up and be your best.

I Could Do Anything If Only I Knew What It Was: How to Discover What You Really Want and How to Get It, by Barbara Sher (Dell Trade Publisher). Barbara is a great writer and bestselling author of *Wishcraft.* She address emotional barriers such as fear of success and pleasing others. This is an easy read for those who want to challenge themselves to achieve their dreams.

Create You and Co.: Learn to Think Like the CEO of Your Own Career, by William Bridges (Perseus Books).

Be Your Own Brand: A Breakthrough Formula for Standing Out from the Crowd, by David McNally and Karl D. Speak (Berrett-Koehler Publishers). This book focuses on the individual, with an emphasis on defining what you offer that's of value to others. It includes good value clarification exercises.

Finding Your Perfect Work: The New Career Guide to Making a Living, Creating a Life, by Paul and Sarah Edwards (Tarcher). As self-employment experts, the authors of this book provide information for independent consultants who want to clarify their gifts, mission, passion, and personal assets and put them to work as entrepreneurs.

On Careers

The Three Boxes of Life and How to Get Out of Them, by Richard N. Bolles (Ten Speed Press). You will not find more resources and ideas anywhere else than are in this book for exploring your career and making decisions about what to do next. Bolles covers it all—from graduating to career change. This book is dense with ideas and actions you can take. I find it almost too much!

What Color Is Your Parachute, by Richard N. Bolles (Ten Speed Press). This is a classic for job hunters and career changers. He helps you find a job that's right for you and teaches you how to create opportunities.

Whistle While You Work, by Richard J. Leider and David Shapiro (Berrett-Koehler Publishers). Comfortable and relaxing to read, this book softly challenges you to focus on your passion and find your calling. The authors stress the importance of purpose and visions and encourage you to discover your calling.

On Leadership

Good to GREAT: Why Some Companies Make the Leap . . . and Others Don't, by Jim Collins (HarperCollins Publishers). This book has terrific stories about great organizations that are taking time to "get the right people on the bus." Collins communicates the value of recruiting a great leadership team and lining up employees who can deliver.

Love 'Em or Lose 'Em: Getting Good People to Stay, by Beverly Kaye and Sharon Jordan-Evans (Berrett-Koehler Publishers). This is absolutely the best book on the market for learning A to Z strategies on how to keep your best employees.

The Rise of the Creative Class, by Richard Florida (Basic Books). This is a must-read about the changing demographics worldwide and the implications for business.

The World Is Flat, by Thomas L. Friedman (Farrar, Straus and Giroux). This is a mind-bending book about the shift from horizontal to vertical leadership and the need to play a new game.

A Whole New Mind: Moving from the Information Age to the Conceptual Age, by Daniel Pink (Penguin Group). Daniel Pink is a forward thinker who charts out the type of work that's evolving in organizations today.

On Teamwork

Get Everyone in Your Boat Rowing in the Same Direction: 5 Leadership Principles to Follow So Others Will Follow You, by Bob Boylan (Adams Media). This is a fun book that's easy to read. There are lots of cartoons and images as well as solid ideas to help leaders get on the same page and head in the same direction.

On Trust

Trust and Betrayal in the Workplace, by Dennis S. Reina and Michelle L. Reina (Berrett-Koehler Publishers). Dennis and Michelle are probably the first consultants to do hard-core research on the behaviors that build trust. They are both practical and researched based.

Built On Trust: Gaining Competitive Advantage in Any Organization, by Arky Ciancutti, M.D., and Thomas L. Steding, Ph.D. (Contemporary Books). The authors talk eloquently about "getting out of the muck." There are good descriptions of real situations and how to unravel them with finesse by gaining closure and commitment.

Trust in the Balance: Building Successful Organizations on Results, Integrity, and Concern, by Robert Bruce Shaw (Jossey-Bass Publishers). Shaw offers valuable, short assessment tools in his book on aspects of trust such as "showing concern, exhibiting trust behaviors, focusing on results, and demonstrating integrity."

On Organizational Culture

First, Break All the Rules: What the World's Greatest Managers Do Differently, by Marcus Buckingham (Simon and Schuster). Gallop is the leader in research and data on people management. All the Gallop books are excellent materials that offer researched-based approaches to leading people, focusing on what's right instead of what's wrong, and creating high-impact cultures.

On Future Trends

Re-imagine! by Tom Peters (Dorling Kindersley Limited). If you want to peek into the future, this book is for you. Written by a "Diamond" mind, he blitzes you with facts and ideas, and he challenges you to wake up and see what's happening to middle-management jobs, women in the workplace, and changing customer perspectives. It is an excellent resource for a wide-angle view of work and the changes afoot.

On Communication

Brag! The Art of Tooting Your Own Horn Without Blowing It, by Peggy Klaus (Warner Business Books). I love the title of this book and the sassy way it's written. It is excellent for encouraging you to speak up and speak out about what you do best! This book tells you how to brag without being obnoxious.

Difficult Conversations: How to Discuss What Matters Most, by Douglas Stone (Viking Press). This is an excellent guide to initiating and completing difficult conversations. This book lives up to its title by offering real-time guidelines and phrases to help you tackle tough issues.

Fierce Conversations: Achieving Success at Work & in Life, One Conversation at a Time, by Susan Scott (Viking Press). Scott excels at recognizing the dynamics that go on beneath the surface during difficult conversations. She appreciates the challenges involved and offers practical phrases and steps to walk into difficult waters.

The Adversity Quotient at Work: Finding Your Hidden Capacity for Getting Things Done, by Paul G. Stoltz (Harper Business). I love this book. My daughter-in-law loaned it to me and I never gave it back. Stoltz deals with the underbelly of resistance and how to think differently in order to get things moving in the right direction. It is a must-read.

Index

About the Author

FAITH RALSTON, PH.D., is an expert consultant and trusted advisor to key business leaders. Her organization, Leaps of Faith, Inc., helps leaders build trust and leverage everyone's talents to achieve their vision. Faith is an inspirational speaker with twenty-five years' experience of working with leaders and teams in *Fortune* 500 corporations and large organizations.

Clients include American Express, Andersen Windows, BlueCross BlueShield of Minnesota, Cadbury Schwepps, Deluxe Check, Fortis Insurance, General Mills, Graco, Hewlett Packard, Honeywell, IBM, Medtronic, PricewaterhouseCoopers, Sandia National Laboratories, and hundred of others.

Faith is the author of several books and the creator of Play to Your Strengths Talent System, which has helped thousands of leaders and teams leverage their talents to achieve their vision. Her unique 360 Talent Assessments help every individual bring their best to the organization.

Faith's articles have been published in syndicated newspapers and magazines and she has been featured in the *Chicago Tribune, Star Tribune, City Business*, and *Pioneer Press*. Faith has a Ph.D. in adult development, an M.A., in counseling psychology, and a B.A. in English. She is the mother of four incredible sons—who are living proof of strengths in action.

Sign up for Faith's Bold Leader's newsletter at *www.playto yourstrengths.com* and receive a free copy of the Discover Your Talents assessment.